The Fifteen Minute Hour

The Fifteen Minute Hour

Applied Psychotherapy for the Primary Care Physician

Marian R. Stuart, Ph.D.
Joseph A. Lieberman III, M.D.

PRAEGER

New York
Westport, Connecticut
London

Library of Congress Cataloging-in-Publication Data

Stuart, Marian R.
  The fifteen minute hour.

  "Praeger special studies. Praeger scientific."
  Includes bibliographies and index.
  1. Physician and patient. 2. Sick — Psychology.
3. Psychotherapy. 4. Family medicine. I. Lieberman,
Joseph A. (Joseph Aloysius), 1938-   II. Title.
[DNLM: 1. Family Practice. 2. Primary Health Care.
3. Psychophysiology. 4. Psychotherapy. WM 420 S9315f]
R727.3.S87   1986   610   86-80
ISBN 0-275-92022-4 (alk. paper)
     0-275-92598-6 (pbk.)

Copyright © 1986 by Praeger Publishers

All rights reserved. No portion of this book may be
reproduced, by any process or technique, without the
express written consent of the publisher.

Library of Congress Catalog Card Number: 86-80
ISBN 0-275-92598-6

First published in 1986

Praeger Publishers, One Madison Avenue, New York, NY 10010
An imprint of Greenwood Publishing Group, Inc.

Printed in the United States of America

The paper used in this book complies with the Permanent
Paper Standard issued by the National Information Standards
Organization (Z39.48-1984).

10 9 8 7 6 5 4

Acknowledgments

The authors wish to recognize and express appreciation to the many people who made meaningful contributions to this book. We would first like to thank the following physicians: Hana Chaim, D. O.; Alicia Dermer, M. D.; Joan Gopin, M. D.; Patricia Janku, M. D.; Naomi Kolb, M. D.; Ronald Lau, M. D.; Yves Morency, M. D.; Jean Plover, M. D.; Andrew Sachere, M. D.; Roger Thompson, M. D.; and Harvey Weingarten, M. D. for practicing our methods and contributing experiential clinical material. We would also like to acknowledge our colleagues: Robert C. Cassidy, Ph. D; Joseph Cohn, M. D.; Robert Like, M. D.; Frank C. Snope, M. D.; and David Swee, M. D. for the suggestions, elusive references, and encouragement they supplied. Finally, we would like to thank Louise Ignoscia, Joan Roberts, and Pam Seales without whose goodwill and support our deadlines could not have been met.

Contents

Acknowledgments — v

Introduction — 1

CHAPTER

1. The Relationship Between Mental and Physical Health: Implications of the New Medical Model — 5

2. How Patients React to Stress — 19

3. The Psychotherapeutic Qualifications of the Primary Care Physician — 37

4. Basic Principles and Strategies of Psychotherapeutic Change — 55

5. Differences in Approach to Therapy Between the Primary Care Physician and the Psychiatrist — 80

6	The Structure of Therapy	101
7	Rationale and Techniques for Fifteen Minute Therapy	115
8	Contents of the Fifteen Minute Therapy Session	132
9	Handling Special Patients and Situations	152
10	Anticipated Outcomes	174
Appendix	A Dozen Good Questions and Three Good Answers for All Seasons	189

Index   191

About the Authors   199

Introduction

This book has only one purpose. It is to convince you that by routinely incorporating psychotherapeutics into medical practice, many problems may be solved and/or prevented. The book grows out of our own clinical practice and experience in training residents and practicing physicians in the art of therapeutic talk.

There are several things that this book is not. It is not a book on psychiatry in primary care. There are several good books that deal with that subject. It is not a book on dealing with mental illness or on its diagnosis. It is not a text on psychoanalysis. This is a book on incorporating useful knowledge from broad fields of psychology and psychotherapy into medical practice in order to become more effective in dealing with the emotional overlay or underlay of problems that patients bring to the primary care physician.

We hope that we can demonstrate the importance of dealing with the psychological components related to the patient's health status. We would also hope that you will master the relatively simple techniques that we advocate for dealing effectively with this dimension of patient care. If you have already accepted responsibility for managing the psychosocial problems brought by patients, or if we can convince you to do so, then this book will provide you with theoretical background material that we hope will be extremely useful. We will point out what actually works in practice to help improve patients' functioning. Further, we will provide specific suggestions, outlines for therapy, and particular phrases and approaches that we have developed, practiced, taught, and tested over the last seven years.

Our way is not necessarily the only true, good, or beautiful way to engage patients in therapy, but it is a flexible, practical approach that is easily learned, and it works! Also, it is designed to fit into a regular fifteen minute (or less) office visit without requiring lengthy, extended therapy sessions.

We recommend that you read this book from the beginning to the end. Early chapters provide the theoretical background and rationale for the subsequent chapters, which focus on just what to do and how to do it.

In essence, this is a how-to book. We aim to help you develop skills that will help both you and your patient. We will provide some tools that you can use in your practice. They are effective tools that require less investment of time and energy than you would imagine. We will explain the tools and exactly how to use them.

There are many schools of psychotherapy. We are not preaching a dogma, but invite you to experiment and practice the techniques that we are promoting and empirically establish their usefulness for yourself. We do not wish to establish a true religion in this area. We are quite comfortable with practical eclecticism because it works, and primary care physicians desperately need techniques that work. In essence what we are saying is "Try it, you'll like it."

Over 100 years ago, John Godfrey Saxe, a Vermont poet, lawyer, and humorist, wrote the following poem, "The Blind Men and the Elephant,"[1] which was based on an Indian tale thought to date back thousands of years. It still seems most applicable today.

> It was six men of Indostan
>   To learning much inclined,
> Who went to see the Elephant
>   (Though all of them were blind)
> That each by observation
>   Might satisfy his mind.
>
> The *First* approached the Elephant,
>   And happening to fall
> Against his broad and sturdy side,
>   At once began to bawl:
> "God bless me! but the Elephant
>   Is very like a wall!"
>
> The *Second*, feeling of the tusk,
>   Cried, "Ho! what have we here
> So very round and smooth and sharp?
>   To me 'tis mighty clear
> This wonder of an Elephant
>   Is very like a spear!"

The *Third* approached the animal,
  And happening to take
The squirming trunk within his hands,
  Thus boldly up and spake:
"I see," quoth he, "the Elephant
  Is very like a snake!"

The *Fourth* reached out an eager hand,
  And felt about the knee
"What most this wondrous beast is like
  Is mighty plain," quoth he;
"'Tis clear enough the Elephant
  Is very like a tree!"

The *Fifth* who chanced to touch the ear,
  Said: "E'en the blindest man
Can tell what this resembles most;
  Deny the fact who can,
This marvel of an Elephant
  Is very like a fan!"

The *Sixth* no sooner had begun
  About the beast to grope
Then, seizing on the swinging tail
  That fell within his scope,
"I see," quoth he, "the Elephant
  Is very like a rope!"

And so these men of Indostan
  Disputed loud and long,
Each in his own opinion
  Exceeding stiff and strong,
Though each was partly in the right,
  And all were in the wrong!

In our opinion different schools of psychology and psychiatry use different glasses with which to view the patient and the patient's problems. Each has something valuable to offer. Each has a small piece of useful insight. Collectively, these fragments form a practical armamentarium with which to help people suffer less, be less vulnerable to physical and psychological ills, and more productive in structuring satisfying lives for themselves and their loved ones.

In writing this book we have tried to present a coherent whole. Each chapter builds on the previous one, although we have incorporated illustrative clinical examples all through the text. The case material is based entirely on actual encounters, although we have changed the names, and altered some details in order to guarantee patients' confidentiality.

In Chapter 1, we discuss current trends in the delivery of health care, the outmoded medical model, and the need to employ a new structure that integrates George Engel's biopsychosocial model with an awareness of current sociological, political, and economic realities. Chapter 2 presents in detail patients' reactions to stress and forms the theoretical basis for the effectiveness of the type of therapy that we are promoting. We bring research findings from a variety of sources, some of which may be new to you, and try to build a strong case. In Chapter 3 we discuss the qualifications and natural proclivity that primary care physicians have that make them ideal psychotherapists.

In the following chapter we present, from a variety of viewpoints, what we consider to be the actual elements that induce the type of positive changes that we attribute to psychotherapy. We deal with elements common to all schools of psychotherapy and introduce the reader to some specific modalities that we feel are particularly useful. Chapter 5 looks at the differences between the type of psychotherapy we are advocating and that which is generally provided by traditional mental health practitioners. Again, the second part of this chapter falls into the how-to category, as we suggest ways of applying these differences.

Chapter 6 focuses on how to structure the therapy, and Chapters 7, 8, and 9 provide clear directions on just what, how, and when to do what we propose and with whom. Chapter 10 will bring the reader full circle into the present and the future.

We hope you will enjoy reading this book. Please, have fun with it. Your patients will love you.

Marian R. Stuart, Ph.D.
Joseph A. Lieberman III, M.D.

REFERENCE

1. Saxe, John G. *Clever Stories of Many Nations: Rendered in Rhyme.* Boston: Ticknor and Fields, 1865.

The Relationship Between Mental and Physical Health: Implications of the New Medical Model

1

American medicine, always in evolution, now faces changes the magnitude of which have never before been encountered. Among the many reasons for this are the dramatic proliferation of knowledge in general, the effects of burgeoning technology, sociological changes within the community that encourage wellness and self-help programs, redirection of financial resources with material constraints imposed on both the public and private sectors, and increased longevity with its concomitant chronic illness. Each of these phenomena in their own way are working to reshape the American health care delivery system.

All of this ferment can be very distressing, ominous, and uncomfortable for the physician, while at the same time, it can be challenging, and, in many ways, refreshing. The primary task that must be undertaken is to find a successful way of adapting to the changing circumstances. The physician who wishes to endure and prosper is now faced with the need to acquire new skills and rethink some ideas that are currently being challenged by others. What is critical is meeting patients' emerging needs. Central to this issue, for the contemporary practitioner, is the ability to understand what these needs are.

It has long been recognized that the first step in solving any problem is to identify the problem. The simple recognition of a situation as a problem alters it. This book will be largely devoted to looking at the doctor-patient relationship and the patients' needs from a somewhat different than traditional perspective. We hope in this way to help define problems that heretofore may have never been considered by the traditionally trained physician. It is precisely in the resolution of these problems that the contemporary practitioner will gain the skills needed to practice medicine effectively in this new, and at times difficult, health care delivery climate.

ECONOMIC CONSIDERATIONS

Not the least of the events behind these changes in medical practice is the restructuring of the financial reimbursement system for medical services. Until recently, the preeminent method of payment of physicians was on a fee for service basis. Typically, a patient would present to a physician with an illness, such as an appendicitis, and a service, in this instance an appendectomy, would be performed by the physician for which a fee was collected from the patient or the patient's insurance carrier. With this method, surgical services, or least those services involving high technology, are generally compensated better than the so-called cognitive services, although both may involve equivalent time and effort on the part of the physician. Such a system, of course, rewards utilization, because there is no payment unless the service is rendered. Likewise, such a system favors the more complicated over the simpler, and the procedural over the cognitive, because in both instances the former is more liberally rewarded financially.

It is interesting to note that patients are frequently the innocent players in this scenario, since they have little choice and no expertise concerning the services they are to receive. With the proliferation of health care insurance, patients now bear little responsibility for the financial consequences of their physicians' actions. Physicians frequently find themselves in the position of being rewarded only if they do something, and being pressured by patients, who, because they have insurance, want something done. Rightly or wrongly, much of the blame for rapidly rising health costs is laid upon this method of reimbursement.

The Great Society of the '60s had, as a cornerstone of its health care philosophy, a dedication to the equalization of access to medical care for all Americans, regardless of age, sex, race, economic status, or geographic location. By the mid '70s, the consensus among government health care planners was that this grand dream was not feasible economically. Subsequently, cost containment for medical expenditures began to drive policy formation and implementation to the public sector.

Recently, private industry, which had played a largely passive role in this entire process, has caught up with our cost-conscious government.

Both parties are now concerned about the amount they must pay to support their respective insurance or entitlement programs. Rather than worry about quality or access to care, government and industry in concert are now almost exclusively oriented to the bottom line. As a result, they are energetically supportive of any programs that can reduce health care costs.

For the primary care physician or generalist in medical practice, this reorientation and redirection of resources presents an opportunity to maximize efforts directed toward such things as preventive medicine and cost effective health care. Systems of reimbursement are now in place that do not pay on a fee for service basis, but rather reimburse the physician by providing the practitioner with a set monetary remuneration for a patient or family over a specified period of time. This form of reimbursement, gaining in popularity, rewards the practitioner who can minimize expenditures such as hospitalization and maximize "wellness." These activities will result in conservation of those funds forwarded for the care of each patient or family. In this book, we will present strategies whereby this can be accomplished by providing effective psychosocial treatment in the context of a standard office medical practice. The strategies that we propose, coupled with good medical practice, should enable the knowledgeable practitioner to maintain a competitive position relative to other practitioners in what is becoming an overcrowded profession. As Paul Starr bluntly pointed out, "Increasingly, the gains of one physician, or group of physicians, will have to come at the expense of other physicians or providers."[1] Farsighted physicians must acquire the skills needed to flourish in just such a professional environment.

THE LIMITS OF THE TRADITIONAL DISEASE-ORIENTED MEDICAL MODEL

To improve our understanding of the need for acquisition of new skills by the contemporary physician, we might start by looking to the past to understand more completely how that physician was trained, meaning how the practitioner acquired the current skills. Traditional medicine has long and effectively concerned itself almost exclusively with the biomedical model of illness. This model creates a structure for examining, classifying, and treating disease. In the process, this pathogenic orientation creates a dichotomous classification of people as either having or not having a disease. Diseases are viewed almost in isolation from their patient victims. This reductionistic approach, which literally separates the patient from the disease, has been the working model in both our health care delivery and medical educational systems. It is the disease itself that is on center stage, and efforts are directed mainly toward categorization of the disease from largely etiological and therapeutic perspectives. The disease is the raison d'être for the doctor/patient encounter and thus, in most instances, dictates an acute care setting for the encounter.

To arrive at the proper etiology, and thereby establish the proper therapy, the reductionistic approach is also utilized in clinical decision making. Diseases are traditionally put into large classifications and then gradually subclassified until the specific disease entity is identified. Further, it is assumed that each disease has a specific cause for which treatment, in one form or another, is generally available. Frequently, the choice between chemical, surgical, radiological, or other treatment must be made, but always with the intention of somehow counteracting the cause of the pathology and thereby changing the natural course of the disease. The main function of the traditional physician has been to work through this process with the patient and prescribe an appropriate therapy when an etiological diagnosis is established.

This type of clinical reasoning lends itself particularly well to the generalist's need for a system for approaching an undifferentiated patient population. By this we mean the need for a model that will enable the primary care physician to deal effectively with a waiting room full of patients who have varying and unorganized signs, symptoms, and problems. Frequently, these patients have few external clues as to what may be the nature of their particular problem. While individually they may be suffering from a variety of problems, collectively their problems are even more poorly defined. Categorization, followed by subcategorization, and then sub-subcategorization, efficiently leads one from these broad-based, frequently ill-defined presenting problems to a manageable diagnostic entity that is then amenable to specific therapeutic intervention. The physician, in an efficiently organized fashion, is able to sort through a variety of data and arrive at a meaningful conclusion that dictates a specific action.

There is a real problem with the above scenerio. Although it certainly works in clarifying issues for the physicians, we agree with George Engel[2] that:

The crippling flaw of the model is that it does not include the patient and his attributes as a person, as a human being. The biomedical model can make provision neither for the person as a whole nor for data of a psychological or social nature, for the reductionism and mind-body dualism on which the model is predicated requires that these must first be reduced to physiochemical terms before they can have meaning. Hence, the very essense of medical practice perforce remains "art" and beyond the reach of science.

It would seem that the biopsychosocial sum is greater than the whole of the biomedical parts. That not withstanding, this model is still the preeminent way in which contemporary American medicine is practiced. A better understanding of this process can be achieved by an examination of its application in its most common form, the typical office encounter.

THE NATURE OF THE OFFICE VISIT

Under ordinary circumstances, patients present themselves at the doctor's office with a symptom or collection of symptoms. The physician goes through a series of physical assessments and laboratory and other evaluations and then arrives at a working hypothesis as to the cause of the patient's symptomatology and, therefore, the nature of the patient's disease. After developing a differential diagnosis, listing all the disease entities that might account for the symptoms, the physician uses the data collected to rule out the most serious diseases, in this manner arriving at a diagnosis that provides a label for the patient's condition. The appropriate therapy is then prescribed. Quite commonly, this is of a pharmacological variety and, therefore, at this juncture, the prescription is frequently generated. In fact, the issuing of the prescription consistently marks the end of the doctor/patient encounter. If no pathological cause can be established for the patient's symptoms, the diagnosis is frequently made that these symptoms are some manifestation of a psychiatric disorder. Again the prescription is employed. However, on this occasion, a psychotherapeutic agent is frequently used. Nonetheless, the encounter is still terminated in the traditional fashion, by the issuing of the prescription. Central to this process is the implication that every disease must have a specific cause and that, in the main, these causes can be pharmacologically treated. If a definite cause cannot be ascertained, then at least the symptoms can be treated, also pharmacologically.

The office encounter is now almost complete. The patient is expected to pay for the visit, or at least sign the insurance form attesting to having received specific services.

THE TENSION BETWEEN THE SCIENTIFIC METHOD AND PATIENTS' NEEDS

Regrettably, this entire scenerio frequently meets the needs of the physician far better than those of the patient. Perhaps this is the problem that is central to the issue. Patients arrive at the physician's office knowing only that they do not feel well and have symptoms. After a series of maneuvers and studies, patients are informed of a purported cause for their symptoms. If this is amenable to a specific therapy, they will be fortunate enough to have their symptoms relieved and be considered cured. The physician is gratified that the patient can, in fact, be treated and the patient is equally satisfied that the particular problem has been dealt with effectively. The patient is very grateful. Far more commonly, however, the patient's symptoms are part of a much larger gestalt. Patients are multidimensional and bring many problems to the physician, some of which are quite obvious while many others take the form of hidden agenda. McWhinney suggests that if the "patient is fortunate, he will find a physician who will meet these needs as well as providing the best of technical care."[3] The physician needs to be a student of human nature if the underlying reasons for a patient's visit are to be discerned. However, if the physician simply focuses on the organic aspects that are presented, it is likely that this unidimensional view will not allow an accurate perception of the patient's problem(s).

The presenting problem, which the physician can frequently handle with little difficulty, on many occasions is not the main reason for the patient's visit. There is a substantial body of literature showing that persons do not visit doctors simply for relief of organic disorders, but also go to the primary care physician because of life stress, psychiatric disorders, social isolation, and informational needs.[4] Even those patients who are fortunate enough to have their symptoms relieved by the physician's intervention may find this insufficient to meet all of those other needs. If, on the other hand, patients have the misfortune of not even having their symptoms relieved and are informed that, in fact, it is "only your nerves that are causing your symptoms," they are subject to the stigma that this explanation implies. All too frequently, they are only left with therapy that will relieve their most obvious symptoms but not treat the underlying condition. By turning off the symptom, which is a signal that something is wrong, the physician removes the evidence without addressing the problem. By analogy, if we were to turn off the bell on our telephone, we would never know when someone was calling, and therefore we could not respond by either giving or receiving information.

THE RELATIONSHIP BETWEEN PHYSICAL AND PSYCHOLOGICAL HEALTH

Certainly, we cannot totally denigrate the value of the reductionistic approach to the patient, particularly when there is a specific physical malady explaining the symptomatology. But if the physician is truly to be a healer, this approach is far too limited to satisfy the needs of today's patient, even though it may admirably satisfy the needs of the physician. We have alluded on several occasions to the traditional biological approach to the evaluation of symptoms. It should be obvious that we feel that this is inadequate to deal with patient needs.

The inadequacy of this approach is now being substantiated by research. These investigations indicate conclusively that the soma does not function in a vacuum, but rather the psyche and the soma are so closely related that indeed the imbalances of one can produce disease in the other. There is a geometric progression in the production of studies of stress-related disorders. A patient's psychological response to diagnosis and/or treatment of cancer can be related to the course of the disease.[5,6] Greer, Morris, and Pettingale found that women diagnosed as having breast cancer who expressed anger and hostility have a better prognosis than those who passively and helplessly accept their disease.[6] The mechanism involved in the well-known mortality risk following bereavement first reported by Bartrop and his colleagues[7] was replicated in a prospective study published in The Journal of the American Medical Association, where the spouses of women with breast cancer, had their immune systems carefully monitored through in vitro stimulation of lymphocyte function with specific antigens.[8] These researchers found a highly significant suppression of lymphocyte function within one month of the spouses's deaths and were able to determine that this lymphocyte suppression, which lasted for a period of 14 months after bereavement, was not due to preexisting conditions. These investigators concluded that "suppressed immunity following the death of a spouse may be related to the increased morbidity and mortality associated with bereavement."[9] Weiss[10] cites numerous experimental studies that lead to an increased understanding of the mechanisms involved in the development of peptic ulcers and other gastrointestinal pathology. Studies of the pathophysiological links between behavioral factors and cardiovascular disease are also proliferating, as are studies of the behavioral treatment of hypertension.[11] Other studies focus on the role of psychosocial influences on mortality after a myocardial infarction.[12] If the psyche and the soma were not integrally related, none of these effects would occur.

We do not intend to bore the reader by citing research that may be either familiar or else of little interest. We do intend to heighten awareness and indicate the importance of incorporating these understandings into the day-to-day practice of medicine. It does not appear that this generally is how the contemporary physician practices. In his introduction to Norman Cousins' *The Healing Heart*, the cardiologist Bernard Lown writes:

> Although most physicians would not deny that many variables, including psychological factors, influence disease, these are regarded as secondary and largely irrelevant once the basic cause is discovered. For example, when streptococcal upper-respiratory infections are controlled, psychological factors in a child's rheumatic fever are not given serious consideration. . . . Similarly, some physicians would maintain that once the biology of cancer is comprehended, the psychological factors that may govern its progress or modulate its anxiety and pain become but an irrelevant script on ancient scrolls.
>
> The most immutable fact of life is death. It will never be annulled by artifical organs or scientific progress. The days of a human being will ever be finite, and disease and pain will always stalk life's journey. The patient will always require care, sympathetic judgment, and healing. The physician will never be relieved of the responsibility to assuage pain, promote comfort, and instill hope. But there is an additional aspect, relating to the patient's psychobiological constitution, that has powerful self-regulating and self-healing capacities. In ignoring these intrinsic gifts for self-repair, the physician obstructs the amplification of the efficacy of his own scientific methods and impedes the very process of recovery.[13]

THE DECLINE IN THE RELEVANCE OF TRADITIONAL MEDICINE

Regrettably, the failure to recognize all that the relationship between the psyche and soma implies—by relying heavily on the traditional approach—is resulting in meeting fewer and fewer of the needs of an enlightened patient population. This has resulted in a certain public disenchantment with the medical profession and has spurred the growth of many of the self-help and allied programs seen proliferating today. If, indeed, the physician does not answer a patient's needs, then the patient will seek help elsewhere, even if this so-called help may ultimately be to the patient's detriment.

Cults, quacks, vitamin freaks, purges, blood lettings, extreme nutritionalism, and other persuasions in some ways reminiscent of the Dark Ages are flourishing today, in many ways spurred by the public's disenchantment with the medical establishment's inability to meet their individual needs. Certainly, constructive self-help is to be encouraged. Programs to reduce stress, improve physical conditioning, do away with drug, alcohol and cigarette dependency, and maintain ideal height/weight ratios and good physical conditioning are all to be encouraged. What is unfortunate is that much of the lead in these various areas has been taken by the lay public and not by the medical profession per se. Taylor[14] underscores the need for health care providers, whose scientific knowledge dictates a rational approach that promotes living wisely, rather than allowing cultism or financial aspirations of alternative interests to take the lead. Many components of the self-help movement, constructive as they may be, are in fact still another manifestation of the public's dissatisfaction with the medical profession and the perceived inability of the profession to deal with the individual patient and that patient's needs.

Therefore, it behooves those of us who are in the healing professions to begin to look at what we do and critically analyze how well we are providing that for which the public seeks us out. To deal purely with the physical is in almost all instances to deal incompletely with the patient's problems. We must be able to expand our ability to meet the patient's needs, while at the same time conserving our resources so that we may meet the needs of all of our patients.

We need to reconsider at what we do and change the model or paradigm by which we have been operating. Thomas Kuhn's[15] observations led him to suggest that there is a cycle determining scientific revolutions that must occur periodically. Mahoney describes Kuhn's contribution very concisely:

> According to Kuhn, "normal science" is a powerful problem-solving machine dedicated to grinding out the rich harvest of experimentation. As the machine becomes more precise and productive, however, there are increasing probabilities of encountering—or more accurately, recognizing—anomalies. These anomalous pieces of information do not fit the paradigm's conceptual categories and/or predictions and they cannot be assimilated without at least adjusting, if not overhauling, the machine.[16]

Research has brought to light phenomena that simply cannot be fit into the traditional biomedical model. Because of the new information that we have about both patients and disease, it would seem that traditional medicine is certainly in the crisis stage. We must shift or change the paradigm to build a new structure that accommodates our current understandings and points to effective practice.

Under the old paradigm of medicine, there are seven central concepts.

1. Patients suffer from diseases.
2. Diseases are independent and can be categorized.
3. Each disease has a cause.
4. The physician's task is to diagnose and prescribe.
5. The correct disease can be determined through a process of differential diagnosis.
6. The patient is the passive recipient of this process.
7. The mind and the body are separate entities, although joined by specific psychosomatic diseases.

We have already cited several limits in the traditional medical model. McWhinney[17] pointed out three particular anomalies. The first was the incidence of illness without disease. Studies of abdominal pain have shown that specific diagnoses were obtained in less than 50 percent of cases. Headache, chest pain, back pain, and other illness often present without clear-cut identifiable disease. Second, there is general susceptibility to disease that is evidenced by some patients. Why is it that 25 percent of the patients have 75 percent of the illness? If diseases truly had specific etiologies, then it would seem likely that every person would have an even chance of contracting them. This is not the case. In subsequent chapters we will be discussing some of the factors that make people more or less vulnerable. The third anomaly is, of course, the placebo effect. It cannot be explained using the traditional medical model. In every controlled trial, a percentage of people respond physiologically to an inert substance. The magnitude of the placebo effect varies in every study, but it actually approaches 100 percent in some instances. The difference between treatment and healing has to come from within. The mind as an information- (or belief-) processing organ interacts with the body by producing chemical changes that set up chain reactions in the body.

Perhaps the most important factor in developing a new and more effective medical model is a focus on the process of the doctor/patient relationship and the process of the patient's interaction with the environment. The newly recognized role of the physician is to mobilize the patient's own healing power. Norman Cousins[18] underscores the effectiveness of confidence in the body's recovery potential, involvement in the treatment, and a sense of partnership with the physician as making a major contribution to creating the physiological response involved in healing.

It is quite obvious to us and undoubtedly to any other practitioner who toils in the area of primary care that the old paradigm has in fact been overwhelmed, and that, if a practitioner is to remain relevant, it will be necessary for that practitioner to change the approach taken to the patient. The contemporary practitioner must deal with the paradox that has resulted when training dictates the isolation of an illness by reductionistic approach and yet the patient presents with multiple needs in which the disease entity may play a part of varying importance.

DEVELOPING AN INTEGRATED (HOLISTIC) APPROACH BASED ON THE SCIENTIFIC METHOD

Certainly George Engel's conceptualization of the biopsychosocial model[19] presents an innovative and relevant way to apply the tenets of modern biology and the behavioral sciences to a patient encounter. The biological bases are fully exposed and touched while at the same time the psychosocial context is incorporated.

Engel believes, as we do, and cites Brody,[20] that the basic organic building blocks—that is, subatomic particles, atoms, molecules, up through cell, tissues, organs, and organisms—are part of a larger system, including family, community, subculture, and on up through the biosphere. He further maintains that the systems are interrelated to the degree that an event impacting on any one component of this system has an effect on all other components. He presents clinical examples, such as the stress-related illness of an electrical engineer, producing events in a community, such as loss of income, failure of businesses, and outward migration of the population. In this example, he also demonstrates the impact of stress on the engineer's organ systems with the production of such signs and symptoms as lethargy, pain, nausea, etc. In another example, he refers to the case of severe physical and mental retardation caused by radiation-induced mutation, and he demonstrates how this impact will at the subatomic particle level lead to arrested development in tissues, organs, and systems, cause emotional trauma at the family level, and produce an overall resource strain at the biosphere level.

In both of the examples, Engel cites many other effects that result from the adverse impact sustained predominantly at just one level in this system. We join with him in questioning the wisdom of dissecting out certain levels, such as the cellular, tissue, and organ systems, for study in a reductionistic and isolated fashion. This is characteristically done by the medical profession, leaving the balance of the effects on the total system to other disciplines.

There is a massive, evolving body of literature that substantiates the anecdotal observations of most practitioners who deal with patients day to day. It has been repeatedly noted that many events, far removed from the organ and tissue level, will nonetheless have profound effects on components of the system. Therefore, to study and treat these components in the abstract and to deal with them only in the biomedical context is a form of undertreatment that is every bit as damaging to the patient as undertreatment would be in any other form.

In developing a new, more relevant paradigm of medicine, McWhinney[17] suggested incorporating the following concepts:

1. More attention must be paid to health promotion and disease prevention.
2. We must keep separate disease categories, but recognize the effects of interactions and disease susceptibility.
3. We must pay more attention to nonorganic factors such as environmental and relationship characteristics when determining the etiology of disease.
4. The role of the physician is to mobilize the patient's own healing powers.

5. Physicians must develop advanced communication skills in order to diagnose and treat patients (rather than diseases).
6. Physicians must develop skills to determine the meaning of illness for the patient.
7. The body, mind, and spirit are integrated.

In putting these principles into practice, we plan not only to investigate the patient's psychosocial setting and integrate the psychosocial context into our understanding of the patient's illness, but we also expect to intervene by supporting the patient, tapping into the patient's own resources in a constructive fashion, and thereby optimize outcome.

The traditional reductionistic approach to medical practice has had at its end point an understanding of how a particular disease developed in a given patient. An often-quoted aphorism attributed to Sir William Osler states, "It is much more important to know what sort of patient has a disease than what sort of disease a patient has." Still, that does not tell us exactly what should be done about either the patient or the disease. We intend to spell out clearly how the practitioner can use this information to potentiate a patient's own resources and thereby improve outcome. In the following chapters, we will discuss practical interventions that can be used to achieve these ends.

SUMMARY

The primary care physician is urged to reassess and discard the traditional reductionistic, disease-oriented medical model because of: the dramatic proliferation in medical knowledge, technology, and costs of care; sociological changes within the community that encourage wellness and self-help programs; redirection of financial resources to include prospective payment plans; and autonomous decisions and actions regarding their treatment on the part of the patient population. The typical office visit has generally met the needs of the physician more fully than the multidimensional needs of the patient. Recognizing the interrelationship between physical and psychological health, the true inseparability of the psyche and the soma, and the tension between the scientific method and the patient's needs, the practitioner is urged to focus on the process of the doctor/patient relationship. There is a need to incorporate the insights from George Engel's biopsychosocial model, so as to develop communication skills that will help to foster a therapeutic encounter to support the inherent strength of the patient and promote the patient's own healing powers.

REFERENCES

1. Starr, P. *The Social Transformation of American Medicine.* New York: Basic Books, 1984, p. 424.
2. Engel, G. L. The clinical application of the biopsychosocial model. *The American Journal of Psychiatry*, 1980, *137*, 535-544.
3. McWhinney, I. R. The meaning of holistic medicine. *Canadian Family Physician*, 1980, *26*, 1097.
4. Barsky, A. J. Hidden reasons some patients visit doctors. *Annals of Internal Medicine*, 1981, *94* (part 1), 492.
5. Derogatis, C. R., Abeloff, M. D., and Melisaratos, N. Psychological coping mechanisms and survival time in metastatic breast cancer. *Journal of the American Medical Association*, 1979, *242*, 1504-1508.
6. Greer, S., Morris, T., and Pettingale, K. W. Psychological response to breast cancer: Effects on outcome. *Lancet*, 1979, *13*, 785-787.
7. Bartrop, R. W., Lazarus, L., Luckherst, E., et. al.. Depressed lymphocyte function after bereavement. *Lancet*, 1977, *1*, 834-836.
8. Schleifer, S. J., Keller, S. E., Camerino, M., Thornton, J. C., and Stein, M. Suppression of lymphocyte stimulation following bereavement. *Journal of the American Medical Association*, 1983, *250*, 374-377.
9. Op. cit, p. 374.
10. Weiss, J. M. Behavioral and psychological influences on gastrointestinal pathology: Experimental techniques and findings. In Gentry, W. E. (ed.), *Handbook of Behavioral Medicine.* New York: Guilford Press, 1984.
11. Herd, J.A. Cardiovascular disease and hypertension. In Gentry, W. E., (ed.), op. cit.
12. Ruberman, W., Weinblatt, E., Goldberg, J.D., and Chaudhary, B. S. Psychosocial influences on mortality after myocardial infarction. *The New England Journal of Medicine*, 1984, *311*, 552-559.
13. Lown, B. Introduction to Cousins, N., *The Healing Heart: Antidotes to Panic and Helplessness.* New York: Norton, 1983, pp. 12-13.
14. Taylor, R.B. Health promotion: Can it succeed in the office? *Preventive Medicine*, 1981, *10*, 258-262.
15. Kuhn, T. S. *The Structure of Scientific Revolutions.* Chicago: University of Chicago Press, 1962.
16. Mahoney, M. J. Open exchange and epistemic progress. *American Psychologist*, 1985, *40*, 29.
17. McWhinney, I. Time, Change and the Physician. Plenary Address, Society of Teachers of Family Medicine, Sixteenth Annual Spring Conference, Boston, MA. May 1983.
18. Cousins, N. *The Healing Heart*, op. cit.
19. Engel, G. L. The biomedical model: A procrustean bed? *Man and Medicine*, 1979, *4*, 257-275.
20. Brody, H. The Systems View of Man: Implications for Medicine, Science, and Ethics. *Perspectives Biology and Medicine 17*: 71-92, 1973.

How Patients React to Stress

Neither illness nor health can be understood as purely personal events but must be seen in the context of family and cultural ties. At any given time the patient and the patient's health are influenced by a multitude of factors, including past experience, the present situation, and expectations for the future.[1] We contend—and the central theme of this book is—that simple interventions by the physician can have a major impact on patients' experiences of their illness. The physician can help both patient and family set realistic expectations, minimize the benefit of the *sick role*,[2] and provide social support. By considering the social context as part of the treatment, restoration and maintenance of healthier functioning is enhanced.

STRESS AND SOCIAL SUPPORT

Our understanding of the stress response as a nonspecific physical reaction, a biological mobilization for action, action that is required to adapt to change, comes originally from Hans Selye.[3] There are many ways to define stress and although the reaction of the autonomic nervous system to perceived stress is a standard process, many factors mediate the stress-illness relation. On an individual or psychological level, these include personality traits, coping styles, and social support. Personality traits by definition are set patterns, coping styles may be modified over time, but social support is a resource that can be mobilized by concerned others.

Let us first of all try to define *social support*. Just as every part of the human organism is involved in maintaining homeostasis, so each person also needs to maintain a personal steady state while interfacing with the environment, which means with other people. Some people are more skilled than others in communicating their needs and getting them met. Every person records in memory the subjective experience and interpretation of both the process and outcome of these interactions. This stored information is then used to develop expectations for subsequent encounters. Since these expectations affect the person's manner of interacting with others, these expectations often become self-fulfilling prophecies.

Social support can be understood as a psychological mechanism that provides positive information that helps the individual to reassess or refine perceptions regarding the *quality* of interpersonal relationships. The positive quality of the social support aids the individual in developing more positive expectations toward other people and subsequently behaving in such a manner as to realize them.

A Practical Model

A useful model for understanding how people respond to events is *person plus stress yields reaction*.[4] *Person* refers to the patient's characteristics—demographic data, family influences, previous coping mechanisms, personality structure, genetic predisposition, value systems, and beliefs about the past, the present, and the future.

Stress represents demands on the person. These demands can be internally or externally caused. Internal demands include psychological stress that is self-induced through unrealistic expectations and also physiological stresses, such as hunger, thirst, illness, or perhaps the results of sleep deprivation. External demands may include the demands of other people (which will then be internally processed) or such environmental stressors as noise, heat, or combinations thereof. Stress can be chronic or acute. It can consist of a major event or be the accumulation of daily hassles and petty annoyances that demand attention from the person.[5]

Reaction refers to the person's response to the stress. The primary care physician is consulted because the patient has become uncomfortable with the reactions that can be manifested through a variety of symptoms—physical, emotional, or a combination of both. Sometimes the physician can intervene to reduce the stress, for example, by asking family members to make certain adjustments or writing an excuse to relieve pressures at work. However, it may be more constructive to suggest ways to alleviate the perception of the stress or help the patient develop stress management techniques. In this way, the physician helps the patient to modify the reaction. The stress remains the same. The perception of the stress changes, and the patient reacts differently. *Nothing is changed, but everything is changed.*

HELPING PATIENTS COPE WITH STRESS RELATED TO THE OFFICE VISIT

An appointment with a physician may be stressful for the patient. Negative past experiences with doctors may cause the patient to anticipate unpleasant experiences and arouse the fight/flight response. Since at this point neither fight nor flight is appropriate, unpleasant bodily sensations are experienced.

The patient goes to the doctor because of a physical complaint and/or the anxiety attached to the physical complaint. Current perceptions based on previous encounters with physicians predetermine specific expectations. The patient may feel anxious in anticipation of having to respond to certain demands, such as for personal information or permission to examine parts of the body—physical and emotional exposure. There is really nothing that the physician may not look at, touch, or ask about. There may also be demands to accept the authority of the physician, to try to please the doctor, to follow instructions, to be a good patient. The patient may feel stressed in the dependent role, being out of control in this situation. In this context, a recent study of patients who had been diagnosed as hypertensive showed that 46 percent had significantly lower readings when monitoring their own blood pressure in their own homes.[6]

The Causes of Stress Related to the Office Visit

The causes of stress related to the office visit can be divided into two basic categories. The first has to do with *logistics*, or requirements for the patient to make the appointment, to take time off from work, to get transportation, to arrive and wait and sit in the examining room, and to provide payment. The other category of potential stress concerns the *interpersonal elements* of the visit. Patients may feel stressed as they anticipate questions, scoldings, praise, instructions, and ultimately the diagnosis that the physician might be expected to voice. There are certain demand characteristics[7] that have to do with being a good patient. Some of this is learned behavior on the part of the patient. This learning is greatly influenced by family or cultural perceptions of the "patient role". The physician's expectations regarding the patient's behavior and the patient's expectations regarding the physician's behavior may not always coincide. This may be an additional cause of stress.

By recognizing the effect of the situation on the patient's behavior, the physician can help to relieve stress or anxiety experienced by the patient. Much has been written about the doctor/patient relationship and the necessity for establishing rapport early in the interview. We will suggest key phrases that physicians can use to acknowledge the patient's response to a stressful situation, make it overt, and legitimize or normalize it. As we have said earlier, just recognizing a situation as a problem changes it. By saying to the patient, "It must be difficult for you to get here in the middle of your busy day," or, "You have had to wait a long time and must be quite impatient," the physician helps the patient to relax.

Unfortunately, the physician often explains that he or she has been detained because of six other emergencies or because some other patient was in greater need of attention. This underscores the physician's importance, while minimizing the patient's sense of worth. The lower level of self-esteem makes it increasingly difficult for the patient to cope, thereby increasing stress. These concepts will be discussed further in subsequent chapters.

When we allow that the patient looks upset and that this is a reasonable response given the circumstances, we have given support. One element of support is approval, or at least acceptance, of a person's behavior. In giving support, we give relief. Our aim is always to alleviate the patient's psychological distress. We prefer to manage reactions rather than explain them. As Fritz Perls[8] has emphatically stated, the *what* and *how* is important, not the *why*. It may make little sense to us that patients feel a particular way. However, rather than trying to talk patients out of how they feel or figuring out why they feel that way, we acknowledge those feelings and deal with them in a practical, therapeutic, non-time-consuming way.

Many issues determine expectations in the doctor/patient relationship, such as patient requests and various explanatory models of illness coming out of the patient's cultural heritage.[2,9,10] Full discussion of these elements is beyond the scope of this book, but all are factors that we would subsume under the *person* element of our operational model *person plus stress yields reaction*. In this case, when dealing with the anxiety reaction to the stress of the prospective examination or the anxiety related to the reaction to life stress, it is most important not to say, "You have *no* reason to feel anxious," because if the patient had *no* reason to feel anxious, the patient would *not* be feeling anxious. Instead, it is recommended that the physician say, "I can understand that you would feel anxious in this situation. Let's see what we can do to make you feel better."

WHY PATIENTS ADAPT DIFFERENTLY TO STRESS

When mental health is poor, individuals are more likely to develop disease and are much less tolerant of physical symptoms.[11] The correlation between illness and stressful life events is generally accepted. In 1951, Holmes, Treuting, and Wolff first documented the effects of life situations and the accompanying emotional reactions on patients with hay fever.[12] Holmes and Rahe[13] went on to standardize their schedule of recent life events that has been widely used in research. However, many people under stress do not succumb to disease. These people seem to resist diseases developed by others and seem to prosper both physically and mentally, even under traumatic conditions. What makes them so different?

The Salutogenic Model

In his carefully researched book, *Health, Stress and Coping,* Aaron Antonovsky[14] examines a large body of research to determine what factors seem to protect people from the consequences of stress. He suggests that it is useful to switch from a pathogenic to a salutogenic model when we are studying people's reaction to stress. In determining why some people stay healthy regardless of what happens to them, Antonovsky first lists a variety of generalized resistance resources, such as biogenetic constitutional factors, knowledge/intelligence, education, access to money, and a rational, flexible, and farsighted coping style. Then he points to an orientation to the world that is held by persons who seem most immune to stress-related illness. Antonovsky calls this a sense of coherence, which seems to insulate a person from having negative health consequences, even from stressful events that cause disease in people who are more vulnerable. The sense of coherence is basically a psychological orientation in which individuals are able to make sense out of most aspects of their lives, weaving their experience into a coherent whole. They are able to tie everything to everything else and have a basic faith that, generally things will work out as well as can reasonably be expected, and consider that to be all right. This sense of coherence is an important concept that can be therapeutically applied, as will be discussed later.

It appears to be important to connect aspects of our experience into a coherent whole, just as it is important to feel connected to other people. The lost sense of being connected seems to be critical in feeling and subsequently becoming vulnerable. The mechanism that may be involved in this phenomenon was first proposed by Cassel,[15] who suggested that the subjective interpretation or personal experience of an ill person produces a loss of connectedness. It is the *sensed loss of control* that may make the person more vulnerable by compromising the immune system.

THEORIES ON HOW PATIENTS ADAPT

At this time we would like to look at several sets of research findings. First, let's look at prospective, longitudinal studies that tie mental and physical health.[12,16-18] Next, we will talk about the theoretical and empirical data that indicate that every person has at least two levels of functioning. There is a healthy level that is engaged when the individual feels basically in control and a neurotic level that is engaged when the person feels out of control or unsafe. The feeling of safety is a purely subjective one, which is affected by the person's *locus of control*.[19] *Locus of control* is an important concept that few physicians apply with awareness. A growing body of literature indicates that people's health-related behavior is influenced by their *locus of control*.[20] In connection with feeling safe, individuals with an internal locus of control feel safe when they have the resources (information, power, time) to handle a situation, whereas individuals with an external locus of control feel safe when a trusted authority figure has taken charge and told them what to do or when family or community resources have been recruited for their support. The implications for medical practice and dealing with people under stress are obvious.

The physician who understands the issues involved in these three areas of research will be able to make effective interventions at critical times, with little investment of time, energy, or effort.

A Longitudinal Study of Adaptation

In his book, *Adaptation to Life*, George Vaillant[16] described the details of the lives of a large number of the subjects of the Grant Study of Adult Development, a comprehensive prospective study that followed over 200 initially healthy college men for 40 years. Data were collected through repeated physical examinations and by interviews and comprehensive questionnaires for longitudinal monitoring of psychological, social, and occupational adjustments. All important life events were followed. Among other characteristics carefully studied were the types of symptoms that the subjects developed under stress.

This research clearly demonstrated the connection between healthy psychological and healthy physical functioning. After careful analysis of the data, Vaillant found no evidence to support the existence of specific mental diseases, only evidence of maladaptive reactions to stress.

Vaillant found that people change over time, generally maturing psychologically as they grow older. He also found that some people are healthier than others. Under favorable circumstances, mental health develops and is correlated with robust physical health. This also generally predisposes the person to success in the work environment. Both physical and mental health depend on successful adaptation. In a later report published in the *New England Journal of Medicine*,[11] Vaillant reported that poor physical health accompanied and was followed by poor mental health. Conversely, poor mental health, that is, poor adaptation to stressful life events, was a clear predictor of subsequent poor physical health.[11]

Vaillant, in fact, defines health as *successful adaptation*. It is successfully adapting to problems, not the absence of these stresses, that determines healthy functioning and growth. Vaillant found that individual traumatic incidents did not generally have dramatic effects on the quality of people's lives. Rather, he found that people's lives in general seemed to have a relatively stable course.

By studying the reactions of the Grant Study subjects to the stresses inherent in their lives over 40 years, Vaillant determined a range of adaptive mechanisms, which can equally well be labeled defense mechanisms. He proposed four lines of defenses, psychotic, immature, neurotic, and mature.

Defense mechanisms such as delusional projection, denial, and distortion that are part of the psychotic level are normal for individuals under the age of 5. Immature mechanisms such as projection, hypochondriasis, and acting out are common in healthy 3- to 15-year-olds. The neurotic defenses outlined by Vaillant are intellectualization, repression, and reaction formation, which are commonly seen in "healthy individuals ages three to ninety, in neurotic disorder, and in mastering acute adult stress".[21] Mature mechanisms such as altruism, humor, suppression, anticipation, and sublimation are normal in healthy individuals from 12 to 90. However, under stress they may change to less mature mechanisms. When demands from the internal or external environments become too great for the mature defense mechanisms to handle, the individual temporarily retreats to more primitive defenses. This may be labeled regressing, or under severe conditions it is seen as decompensating.

Extreme stress causes individuals to regress from their characteristic coping mechanisms to poorer or less mature ones. These more primitive coping mechanisms provide less successful adaptation and, therefore, potentiate poorer mental and physical health. Vaillant[16] suggests that it is not stress that kills us, rather that it is ingenious adaptation to stress, which he calls good mental health or mature coping mechanisms, that facilitates our survival. Vaillant's work provides support for the themes that are central to this book:

1. Mental and physical health are inextricably mated.
2. Individuals under stress use different coping mechanisms than they do when they are not under stress.
3. In general, individuals have consistent coping patterns. They use specific patterns at a particular level of maturity under normal circumstances and less functional ones under stress.
4. It is most important to support people under stress to help focus them back onto their more adaptive defenses.

A Holistic Theory of Neurosis

Vaillant comes out of a school of psychoanalytically oriented psychiatry. We will now look at a very differently oriented psychiatrist who provides interesting theoretical support for the conclusions of the Grant study.

Andras Angyal's work is not well known in the medical community. Angyal[22] was a successful analyst who proposed a theory and treatment of neurosis that he labeled a holistic method. His theory is useful because it provides a plausible explanation for the uncomfortable phenomena that people experience when they are under overwhelming stress. Angyal also provides direction for providing relief.

Angyal's theory of human nature and personality posits that two systems, one healthy and one neurotic, vie for dominance in our personality. All persons have a need to feel competent, or as Angyal puts it, there is a drive for autonomy. There is also a companion need to belong, which Angyal calls the need for *homonomy*, essentially a feeling of connectedness. The healthy system develops through the experience of having one's basic needs met, that is, both feeling personally competent and also feeling accepted by the significant others in one's life. It is based on both feeling loved (connected) and effective as an autonomous person. The world of the healthy personality is a reasonably safe and loving place. The neurotic system builds on the experience of feeling incompetent and hateful. It registers only needs that have not been met. Angyal suggests that since no life, however unfortunate, is all trauma, the basic data processed by the two systems is actually the same. Angyal says that we actually live in two worlds. Both are complete systems and they vie for dominance. So since we never live in the world proper, but create our map of the world,[23] not only is *the map not the same as the territory*,[24] but now Angyal is telling us that we actually have two different maps that we use under different circumstances.

We either relate to the world with positive expectations using our healthy map, or fear and discomfort cause us to use our neurotic map. When the neurotic system is engaged, the world seems threatening, hostile, and withholding, and our main aim is to protect ourselves and escape danger. We feel as though the world is too large and we are too small and too inadequate. When caught up in our neurosis, we feel angry, anxious, and isolated. This belief system makes it impossible for us to feel optimistic. We need to feel safe again. Until our healthy self is reengaged, we cannot feel hope or confidence. The role of the supportive person is to restore the sense of trust in the world that is represented by the healthy personality system.

Research from Experimental Psychology

Although shaped in different language, physiological experimental psychology has demonstrated specific responses in subjects under stress.

As people become overaroused (tense and overstimulated), they filter out parts of current experience—coping mechanisms become more primitive in several ways to include reverting to more dominant, first-learned behaviors. Recently learned behavior is not available, so that those responses that would be most appropriate to the situation are temporarily forgotten and cannot be utilized. Novel stimuli are treated as though they were similar to previously experienced ones. When having to cope under highly aroused conditions, people revert to automatic behavior that has been overlearned.[25] When levels of arousal are brought back to a comfortable level, problem solving becomes effective again. The recently learned material again becomes part of the behavioral repertoire, increasing the variety of options available. Mental health is restored.

The connecting thread between these viewpoints confirms our personal clinical experience that under stress people go on *tilt*. For many people, there are degrees of diminishing functioning under stress, perhaps even a peak of efficiency before the decline sets in, but there appears to be a threshold that precipitates behavior that is characteristic of overstressed (overaroused) functioning for each individual. Having passed this threshold, people click in their neurotic map of the world and then act as though that were the only reality. For the physician, the primary therapeutic task becomes providing support that will restore people's equilibrium and refocus them in their healthier orientation. Weik points out that by labeling a problem as minor rather than serious, people's arousal level is lowered. He suggests that this is particularly beneficial when "people don't know what to do or are unable to do it."[26] More will be said about this in later chapters.

Application to Illness Behavior

The effects of acute illness constitute a high degree of stress. Our understanding of the effects on people's behavior under these circumstances can be enhanced by reviewing the normal developmental process by which human beings mature. Writing from the point of view of organizational psychology, Chris Argyris[27] considers five dimensions of individual functioning. He suggests that as people develop they move up along a continuum from being passive to being active; from dependence to independence; from requiring immediate gratification of their needs to being able to delay gratification for long periods; from concrete thinking to abstract thinking; and from having few abilities to having many abilities. Each person functions at a specific level on each of these dimensions. The more highly developed or mature the individual, the higher level of functioning along each axis can be expected. This was confirmed by Vaillant's findings, as discussed earlier. In circumstances of acute stress, people will temporarily regress along each of the five dimensions, though not necessarily to the same extent.

Acute illness is an acute stress. There is an acute regression of functioning. People who are ill become more passive, more dependent, want their demands met instantly, become more concrete in their thinking, and have few abilities to help themselves. This can try the patience of the care giver, but can be easier to handle if it is anticipated and time limited. In chronic illness, unfortunately, the regression often becomes permanent. If a physician is aware of this phenomena, efforts can be made to alleviate further stress by setting realistic expectations for the patient while providing support to maximize return to premorbid levels of functioning. But to be effective, one must start at the level where the patient is.

THE RESULTS OF BEING OVERWHELMED

The subjective feeling of being overwhelmed contributes to the objective inability of individuals to function at optimum levels. The perception of not functioning up to par then contributes to the lowering of self-esteem. These feelings can be transient, lasting only several seconds, or constitute the general phenomenological experience of the individual. Sometimes, these negative experiences of the self are specific to particular situations, triggered by events that are symbolically threatening, or they can be precipitated and maintained by traumatic life events or by an accumulation of daily hassles.[5] In actuality, if the subject experiences the event or accumulation of events as stressful, it is stressful. William James first suggested that emotions and their effect on our bodies are objective phenomena that are determined through the subjective experience:

> Our natural way of thinking about these... emotions is that the mental perception of some fact excites the mental affection called the emotion, and that this latter state of mind gives rise to the bodily expression. My theory, on the contrary, is that the bodily

changes follow directly on the perception of the exciting fact, and that our feeling of the same changes as they occur IS the emotion. Common sense says, we lose our fortune, are sorry and weep; we meet a bear, are frightened and run; we are insulted by a rival, are angry and strike. The hypothesis here to be defended says that this order of sequence is incorrect, that the one mental state is not immediately induced by the other, that the bodily manifestations must first be interposed between, and that the more rational statement is that we feel sorry because we cry, angry because we strike, or tremble because we are sorry, angry, or fearful, as the case may be. Without the bodily states following on the perception, the latter would be purely cognitive in form, pale, colorless, destitute of emotional warmth. We might then see the bear, and judge it best to run, receive the insult and deem it right to strike, but we should not actually feel afraid or angry.[28]

When we feel basically in control of the responses we are making to the events happening in our lives and are able to flee, fight, or flow as appropriate, we function at a particular level. As long as the demands of the external environment (other people) and internal environment (expectations of the self) are experienced as manageable, we will continue to function at our customary level. As discussed earlier, once the tolerance for comfortable adaptation has been exceeded, we begin to use a different coping style. At the extreme, Seligman[29] has shown that once people are convinced that events are completely uncontrollable by their own efforts, that their behavior will in no way effect the outcome of a particular situation, they behave in a stereotyped manner that he has labeled "learned helplessness." This is an emotional sequence that involves going through a fear protest stage and then to a helpless-depressed stage. The more out of control the person feels, the more primitive defenses are called into play. Basically this is the person's attempt at managing when overwhelmed.

Each of us can usually identify when we are feeling overwhelmed by examining the behavioral repertoire that we engage. We literally go on *tilt* and we are unable to do anything about it. In many cases, our perception of our behavior, and the lack of ability to contol or at least modify that behavior, exacerbates the feelings of being overwhelmed. When we lose faith in our power to manage at all, we fall into our dependent mode and look to be taken care of. When there is no one there, or when we do not trust the person who is in charge, we become despondent and helpless.

Research has shown that over time this type of stress can contribute to a compromise of the defense systems of the body and lead to subsequent disease.[30] At first, patients are simply aware of symptoms. Literally, they experience signs, bodily responses to dealing with the stress in their lives. These symptoms may include muscle tension that is experienced as back or neck pain. Headaches are common, as is blurred vision. Patients may become aware of a rapid pulse, abdominal pain, breathing difficulties, mood shifts, sweating, tight throat, or have trouble swallowing. Other less-noticeable bodily reactions triggered by the sympathetic nervous system–mediated stress-response syndrome may result in elevated blood pressure, elevated lipid levels, changes in blood sugar, and ultimately compromise of various organ systems.

THE CRISIS INTERVENTION MODEL

Although patients often experience chronic stress, there are specific times when there are acute episodes triggered by a crisis in a person's life. A crisis may be thought of as an environmentally produced situation to which the individual must respond, such as a disaster, an accident, loss of a job, or the death of a loved one. There are also the normal developmental crises (also called transition points) in the life cycle. A situation may be experienced as a crisis because of the individual's perception of the event as threatening to the self in some highly significant way. Physicians may define a crisis as a clinical syndrome, which is accompanied by emotional upset, rise in tension, unpleasant affect, breakdown of coping mechanisms, and disorganized functioning. A crisis may be thought of most simply as the time of greatest change or potential change. It is a time when decisions made will affect the subsequent options available. It is also a time when certain decisions have to be made because the previous *status quo* no longer exists and some adaptive behavior is required.

In explaining the effectiveness of crisis intervention, Gerald Caplan[31] suggests that each person generally functions within a specific range of effectiveness and personal satisfaction. We have seen this empirically demonstrated in the Grant Study. There is a continuum of functioning, from people who are generally very ineffective to those who are well adjusted and adapted and who enjoy living. In general, people are quite static in their level of functioning, regularly fluctuating in a given range as they experience manageable life stress. In a crisis, the overwhelming amount of experienced stress prevents the individual from problem solving in any effective manner, as discussed earlier. There is an overwhelming amount of emotional distress. Since a crisis is defined as the time of greatest change, regardless of the nature or degree of adaptation required, crisis by definition is time limited. Some resolution will occur within a time span of four to six weeks. Having temporarily moved down on the dependency scale, the individual is generally open to receiving help because of the clearly experienced need.

If the resolution of the crisis is favorable, the individual will function at a higher level of adjustment. New coping skills are learned and confidence in the self and others is enhanced. Conversely, if there is no help available or the individual is not able to solve the problem successfully, with or without help, the crisis will still be resolved, but at the cost of subsequent lower level of functioning. People will move down the scale in all five of Argyris's dimensions.

As we have suggested, during the crisis an individual experiences increased dependency feelings, wishes to be helped, and signals this to the environment. One of the most efficient ways of signaling for help in our society is to develop an illness, either an acute illness or the exacerbation of a chronic condition. The visit to the physician is a cry for help and symptom relief. It affords the physician an opportunity to intervene effectively at a time when the individual in crisis is open and highly suggestible.

The goals of crisis intervention are very specific. First is the prevention of dire consequences. In a crisis, the individual is forced to deal with new situations just at a time when the ability to solve problems is compromised. The intervening person can suggest that no decision be made that is not absolutely crucial and that those issues that must be resolved are talked through carefully with a disinterested person. The second goal is to return the individual to a premorbid level of functioning. This can best be done by providing support, as will be discussed later. Expanding the behavioral repertoire and enhancing self-esteem are the other goals of crisis intervention that follow from successful resolution of the crisis.

The physician can provide symptom relief and empathy for the subjective experience of stress. The physician can be supportive by providing information and explanations, exploring options, or simply pointing out that they must exist. Most of all, the physician can encourage new behavior that will help the patient to manage the crisis and regain a better level of functioning with psychological and physical equilibrium restored.

APPLICATION TO THE OFFICE SETTING

Some patients at first seem reluctant to discuss their psychological condition when they seek medical treatment. The following example is quite typical of our practice.

> Mrs. Z. is a 53-year-old schoolteacher who has come to the office for the second time. Her presenting complaint is a sinus problem; she reports having had congestion and severe recurrent headaches for the past three days. Mrs. Z. has a history of chronic sinusitis, but this time she says the symptoms have persisted for a longer time than usual. Mrs. Z. is a well-dressed, reserved white female who appears somewhat anxious to get out of the office. When she is asked about her current life situation, she reluctantly admits that she is working two jobs, is separated from her husband, but that everything is under control. She refuses to give any details of her current situation, and when asked how she feels about her separation she denies that she has any problems and says that she doesn't want to talk about it. Physical exam is normal. The physician then explains to her that sometimes stress and emotional problems have a way of lowering the body's resistance and making physical symptoms persist longer or be more difficult to treat. If these problems are not recognized and dealt with, physical health is compromised. The physician just presents this explanation to help the patient make sense out of both her current situation and her reaction to it. In order to give Mrs. Z. a few minutes to think about it, he leaves the room to get a prescription pad. When he returns, he notices that Mrs. Z. is looking much more relaxed. She says, "Doctor, I really didn't mind you asking me questions about my separation and so forth. It was good that you did. I really have to start dealing with all that stuff." The doctor then schedules her for an appointment in the following week, primarily to talk about her psychosocial situation. She leaves feeling much better.

We have tried to show that the physician in clinical practice is seeing patients at a time when they are feeling vulnerable. Interventions at this time are very effective, both in terms of restoring the patient's equilibrium and potentiating constructive change. Specific techniques and detailed rationale will be discussed in subsequent chapters. The physician is in a unique position to help the patient at an opportune time and is prearmed with a variety of valuable skills, as will be discussed in the next chapter.

SUMMARY

The stress response is a biologically programmed mobilization for action in response to a demand to adapt to changes in the external or internal environments. A model—*person plus stress yields reaction*—is offered to help specify the point of intervention. A person with particular characteristics (personality variables) subjected to particular environmental demands will have a particular reaction. The visit to the physician is triggered by the reaction. Patients also experience stress in regard to the office visit and their interaction with the physician. This can be reduced through specific strategies.

In general, there is a relationship between illness and adaptation to life events. Mental health potentiates physical well-being. Some people are characteristically healthier than others. Drawing from a variety of sources, we present two central concepts: one suggesting that individuals generally function at a specific level of adaptation and the other that under severe stress, including physical illness, they temporarily regress to lower levels of functioning.

When individuals are in a state of being overwhelmed, they are unable to function at optimum levels. They go on *tilt* and click in their neurotic map of the world. Social support, which provides information regarding the individual's basic acceptability and competence, is crucial at this time.

The crisis intervention model is useful in specifying the time-limited nature of acute stress. Crises generally resolve within four to six weeks. Through providing support, crisis intervention aims at preventing dire consequences and returning the individual to a premorbid level of functioning, while enhancing self-esteem and subsequent coping abilities. Since physicians generally see patients at a time when they feel vulnerable, an understanding of these mechanisms and provision of a supportive response is highly therapeutic for the patient.

REFERENCES

1. McWhinney, I. R. Beyond diagnosis: An approach to the integration of behavioral science and clinical medicine. *New England Journal of Medicine*, 1972, *287*, 384–387.
2. Kleinman, A., Eisenberg, L., and Good, B. Clinical lessons from anthropologic and cross-cultural research. *Annals of Internal Medicine*, 1978, *88*, 251–258.
3. Selye, H. *The Stress of Life*. New York: McGraw-Hill, 1957.
4. Stuart, M. R. and Mackey, K. J. Defining the differences between crisis intervention and short term therapy. *Hospital and Community Psychiatry*, 1977, *28*, 527–529.
5. DeLongis, A., Coyne, J. D., Dakof, G., Folkman, S., and Lazarus, R.S. Relationship of daily hassles, uplifts, and major life events to health status. *Health Psychology*,, 1982, *1*, 119–136.
6. Laughlin, K. D., Sherrard, D. J., and Fisher, L. Comparison of clinic and home blood pressure levels in essential hypertension and variables associated with clinic-home differences. *Journal of Chronic Diseases*, 1980, *33*, 197–206.
7. Orne, M. T. On the social psychology of the psychological experiment with particular reference to demand characteristics and their implications. *American Psychologist*, 1962, *17*, 776–783.
8. Perls, F. S. *Gestalt Therapy Verbatim*. Moab, Utah: Real People Press, 1969.
9. Mechanic, D. Response factors in illness: The studies of illness behavior. In Jaco, G. (ed.), *Patients, Physicians, Illness: A Source Book in Behavioral Science and Health*. New York: Free Press, 1979.
10. Lazare, A. and Eisenthal, S. A negotiated approach to the clinical encounter I: Attending the patient's perspective. In Lazare, A., ed., *Outpatient Psychiatry*. Baltimore: Williams & Wilkins, 1979, pp. 157–171.
11. Vaillant, G. E. Natural history of male psychologic health: Effects of mental health on physical health. *New England Journal of Medicine*, 1979, *301*, 1249–1254.
12. Holmes, T. H., Treuting T., and Wolff, H. G. Life situations, emotions and nasal disease: Evidence on summative effects exhibited in patients with "hay fever." *Psychosomatic Medicine*, 1951, *13*, 71–82.
13. Holmes, T. H. and Rahe, R. H., The social readjustment rating scale. *Psychosomatic Medicine*, 1967, *11*, 213–218.
14. Antonovsky, A. *Health, Stress, and Coping*. San Francisco: Jossey-Bass, 1979.
15. Cassel, J. The contribution of the social environment to host resistance. *American Journal of Epidemiology*, 1976, *104*, 107–123.
16. Vaillant, G. E. *Adaptation to Life*. Boston: Little, Brown, 1977.
17. LaRocco, J. M., House, J. S., and French, R. P., Social support, occupational stress and health. *Journal of Health and Social Behavior*. 1980, *21*, 202–218.
18. Billings, A. G. and Moos, R. H. The role of coping resources and social resources in attenuating the stress of life events. *Journal of Behavioral Medicine*, 1981, *4*, 139–158.
19. Rotter, J. B. Generalized expectancies for internal versus external control of reinforcement. *Psychological Monographs*, 1966, *80*, (1, whole no. 609).
20. Wallston, B. S., Wallston, K. A., Kaplan, G. D., and Maides, S. A. Development and validation of the health locus of control (HCL) scale. *Journal of Consulting and Clinical Psychology*, 1976, *44*, 580–585.

21. Vaillant, G. E., *Adaptation to Life*, op cit., p. 384.
22. Angyal, A. *Neurosis and Treatment: A Holistic Theory*. New York: Wiley, 1965.
23. Korzybski, A. *Science & Sanity*, 4th ed. Lakeville, CT: International Non-Aristotelian Library, 1958.
24. Bateson, G. *Mind and Nature: A Necessary Unity*. New York: Dutton, 1979.
25. Staw, B. M., Sandelands, L. E., and Dutton, J. E. Threat-rigidity effects in organizational behavior: A multilevel analysis. *Administrative Science Quarterly*, 1981, 26, 501–524.
26. Weik, K. E. Small wins: Redefining the scale of social problems. *American Psychologist*, 1984, 39, 41.
27. Argyris, C. *Intervention Theory and Method: A Behavioral Science View*. Reading, MA: Addison-Wesley, 1970.
28. James, W. *The Principles of Psychology*, Vol. 2. New York: Holt, 1913, pp. 449–450.
29. Seligman, M. E. P. *Helplessness: On Depression, Development, and Death*. San Francisco: Freeman, 1975.
30. Christie-Seely, J. Life stress and illness: A systems approach. *Canadian Family Physician*, 1983, 29, 533–540.
31. Caplan, G. *Principles of Preventive Psychiatry*. New York: Basic Books, 1964.

3
The Psychotherapeutic Qualifications of the Primary Care Physician

Primary care represents a comprehensive and personal approach to patient care that mandates addressing psychological and physical problems in an integrated manner. Whether or not the physician actually invites or desires it, the patient expects the physician to deal comfortably and effectively with emotional problems. It is as though the physician becomes a therapist almost by default.

THE REALITY OF BEING ON THE SPOT

It has become a convention to tell someone that there is both good news and bad news. When we assert that primary care physicians are qualified to practice psychotherapy, there is definitely both good news and bad news. The good news is that patients seem to think that they are. There is an impressive literature that shows that patients clearly consider their personal physician to be their primary source of mental health care.[1-3] Now the bad news! Most physicians do not know that they are qualified and have the skills to do effective psychotherapy, therefore they do not make the simple and effective interventions that are available to them.

Although the literature is sparse and controversial, there have been several studies commenting on the efficacy of psychotherapeutic techniques in primary care.[4-9] There seems to be general agreement that the provision of psychotherapy by the primary care physician is considered to be appropriate by both patient and physician, but controlled randomized trials are difficult to do. In one successful study, psychotherapy proved acceptable to both physician and patient, but the rigid protocol requiring exactly 8 one-half hour sessions, no psychiatric referrals, and no medications other than benzodiazepines cramped the physician's style. The 8-week limit proved ineffective in meeting the needs of patients with persistent psychological symptoms.[4] Another structured program, designed to teach practitioners specific behaviorally oriented treatment for depression, was also unsuccessful.[5] Physicians may or may not be successful with existing modalities of therapy, but there seems to be agreement on the need to develop specific techniques and train primary care physicians to manage patients' psychological problems.[4-9] This is precisely what we would like to address.

Patients do talk to their physicians about their personal problems. Many are disappointed when the physician, after listening for a while, cuts them off without any acknowledgment or resolution. Our experience with residents has been that the physician frequently does not know what to say next or feels that enough time has been spent listening, so he or she returns to the business at hand, specifically the physical symptoms. In spite of this, our impression is that many patients feel much better after talking to their physician even though there may be little conscious awareness on the part of the physician of the therapeutic process in the particular interaction or its impact on the patient. Norman Cousins[10] has written much about the importance of the therapeutic interaction with the physician in promoting feelings of being cared for and potentiating healing. In general, without the awareness of inherent skills and particular strategies, physicians have a hard time dealing with the emotional aspects of patients' lives or illness.

In his recent essay in the *New England Journal of Medicine*, Benjamin[11] asserts that the half-life of current medical knowledge is only about five years and that medical technology is growing exponentially. Although this technological progress is impressive and many physicians may feel overwhelmed in trying to keep up scientifically, Benjamin points out that since the true healing skills are those of communication and caring, physicians need to affirm the healing power of their words. He writes:

> The Greeks divided their healers into three categories: the "knife" doctor, the "herb" doctor, and the "word" doctor. Whereas the Greeks held them in balance, the low status today of the "word"

doctors—the psychiatrists—indicates that we believe words are cheap if not useless. We are action oriented and get paid for performing procedures rather than for being—for doing rather than for talking. Western medicine, following the Cartesian dualism between mind and body, has become largely a somatic business. Words have been left behind in the rush to master chemistry. Emotions have been minimized in the reductionist effort to understand cells and genes.

All physicians, whatever their specialty, can improve their therapy of the word. . . . The emotional condition of a patient is as basic as any single factor in the treatment of disease.[12]

It has become clear that the separation of mind and body, as suggested in Chapter 1, has become an anachronistic paradigm. Since all physical illness has an emotional component, the physician is called upon to respond in one way or another. We propose that this response should be handled efficiently, effectively, and comfortably. Also, it should promote healing. It is the healing dialogue between the physician and the patient, addressing the emotional component of the patient's illness, that constitutes the essense of psychotherapy.

PSYCHOTHERAPEUTIC QUALIFICATIONS OF THE PRIMARY CARE PHYSICIAN

What are the characteristics of a therapeutic relationship? Let us look at a few of the more obvious factors.

Trust

The sine qua non of any therapeutic relationship is trust. By trust we mean that the patient has confidence in the integrity, ability, and character of the physician. Because of this confidence, the patient feels free to expose certain personal aspects to the physician with the expectation that these will be respected, honored, understood, and kept confidential. The patient certainly is not aware of the exact text, but knows that the physician is bound by the Hippocratic oath:

> Things that I may see or hear in the course of the treatment or even outside of treatment regarding the life of human beings, things

which one should never divulge outside, I will keep to myself holding such things unutterable (or "shameful to be spoken").[13]

There is also the expectation that the physician will use available training and skill in the patient's interest. In other words, the patient believes in the ability and desire of the physician to provide care. Trust also implies that patients feel assured that no harm will come from disclosing data about themselves, their lives, or that of their significant others to the physician. There is also the expectation that the patient will not be rejected or abandoned.

For trust to develop, a past history of successful encounters with this or other physicians is helpful. In this connotation, *successful* suggests that patients felt better after their encounters with physicians than they did before their visits. It is, of course, possible that trust can be expected without having previously been experienced, such as in the case where a significant other who is trusted (mother) tells someone (son), "The doctor will take care of it." This provides trust by association. These factors, singly and in concert, denote trust. The patient expects to feel safe in the presence of the wise physician who is assumed to be committed to providing personal, ongoing, quality care, and keep strict confidentiality.

Continuity

In primary care, an assumption is made that the physician's commitment to the patient has no defined end point.[14] The continuity of the relationship is thereby established. The personal physician does not treat the patient for just one episode of illness, but expects to follow the patient and attend to the patient's ongoing medical care. If the physician has known the patient and the patient's family over time, this simplifies the communication of particular aspects of any situation. The physician is familiar with the family structure, cultural background, orientation toward physicians, and degree of cooperation that can be expected. The physician already knows many of the factors involved in the patient's personal situation and can be brought up to date quickly. There is also the history of this particular patient's care-seeking behavior. Further, because of the continuity in the relationship, the physician can anticipate and follow critical transitions in the patient's life and intervene in a timely and convenient fashion. The salient point here is that the relationship is preestablished. Even in a group practice, HMO, or a prepaid plan, the patient belongs there. The records have been kept and provide continuity even if a different physician is seeing the patient. There is an expectation of consistent care and follow-up in the particular office, even if it is not with the same physician. The patient cannot be abandoned or rejected.

Nurturance

Competent adults are capable of taking care of themselves and others who are dependent. However, when we are feeling down, besieged, and somewhat overwhelmed by physical or mental stress, we may feel as though we need nurturance. The more depleted we feel by the forces impinging on us, the more dependent we become. At this time, nurturance from others becomes an emergent need. By profession, physicians are seen as healers who provide care and nurturance on demand. This is the expectation that is brought by the patient and is generally met. As discussed in Chapter 1, the patient always gets something from the physician. The prescription or written excuse becomes the symbol of the nurturance that the patient seeks. In any case, the patient asks for help and is open to receive whatever quality of help the physician is ready to provide. Since there is a positive expectation, there will be little resistance to experiencing the positive impact of quality caring. The patient assumes that the physician's training, intelligence, experience, and general wisdom will be devoted to the task of alleviating the patient's pain.

THE ISSUE OF POWER

Although physicians are generally very aware of their power to affect life and death by the medical decisions they make, especially in the hospital setting, few physicians have been exposed to the literature on social power and have little awareness of their powerful potential to influence other people's attitudes and behavior.

What Is Social Power?

Social power has been defined as the potential that one person has to change the beliefs, attitudes, or behavior of another person.[15] Changing a patient's beliefs, attitudes, or behavior is the essence of psychotherapy. Basically, power can be defined as the ability to satisfy someone's needs. If we can satisfy our own needs, we have personal power. We have enough resources that we are not dependent on other people. If we can satisfy other people's needs, then we have power over them. We can reward their appropriate behavior or withhold rewards when their behavior is not to our liking. Learning theory underscores the process by which behavior is modified in response to being rewarded (reinforced). When one person has the potential for inducing forces that will move another person toward acting or changing in a particular way, that person is said to have power over the other person.

Nobody Does Nothing for Nothing

Social exchange theorists see all human relationships in terms of potential payoffs.[16] Using this framework, all interpersonal relationships are seen as exchanges of behavior between people. Great stress is placed on the ability to provide rewards that cause behavior to be repeated. Exchange theory takes a common sense approach that suggests that people only relate to other people because they get something out of it. Even expertise is seen as a commodity.[17] Those people who have commodities to trade have power. In this connection, Postman[18] points out that to a large extent the authority that adults have over children derives from their being the principle source of knowledge. Bacon[19] was quite accurate when he asserted, "Knowledge is power." Physicians have a great deal of knowledge at their disposal that they can apply to relieve the distress of their patients. However, this knowledge is only one source of the physician's power. Before we examine the many power resources at the disposal of the physician, it will be useful to distinguish between the concepts of attributed and manifest power.

Attributed versus Manifest Power

When we say that we give someone power that generally implies that we hold them in high esteem and allow them to influence our behavior and our feelings. Social psychologists distinguish between *attributed* power and *manifest* power. Power is attributed to someone who is judged by others to have the potential ability to influence them. It is assumed that the person has certain resources that can be provided or withheld. When we talk about manifest power that means that the ability to induce behavior change in others has been clearly demonstrated. There is a history of having successfully influenced others' behavior. Physicians have both types of power. They are given a great deal of attributed power. Patients respect them—sometimes even fear them—and expect to be influenced by them. Physicians clearly have manifest power—this is demonstrated through giving prescriptions, writing excuses, filling out insurance or disability forms, doing procedures, ordering tests or hospitalizations, and reporting contagious diseases, to mention only a few examples.

The Mechanisms of Changing Attitudes

Changing attitudes of other people generally requires a different sort of power connotation than changing behavior. Kelman[20] distinguishes three different mechanisms involved in interpersonal influence: internalization, identification, and compliance. Because this material is so rarely made available to physicians and because it is so extremely valuable in a practical sense, we will go into some detail. Kelman[20] suggests that when we look at attitude change we must consider three different parameters: cognitive, affective, and conative. Cognitive factors relate to the belief system of the person. Affective factors relate to the emotions that are aroused by the situation. And conative factors determine what efforts the person will make to act on the redirected principles.

The conative parameter is affected most by power as outlined in the previous section. What we are talking about here is the power to apply rewards or punishment, which leads to compliance. It is manipulating behavior. People act because they feel they have to, and the behavior will cease when the contingencies are removed. The affective parameter is influenced by the attractiveness of the power source, leading to identification. What this means is that because the person to be influenced is positively affected by the person who is suggesting change, the desire to be like (or liked by) that person induces the new orientation. The credibility of the power source acts in the cognitive parameter, leading to internalization of information. People change their beliefs because they are convinced by information that is at first different from their current understanding but presents a convincing picture because of the qualifications of the source providing the new information.

It can be seen that the physician is at once a powerful, attractive, and credible source of information. The physician's potential for effecting permanent attitude change in patients is great. This potential can be judiciously and practically applied in the therapeutic interview.

The Five Types of Social Power

Having defined social power and looked at some parameters of the ability to change attitudes, we would like to elaborate further on outcomes of research regarding social power. We contend that physicians are not accurately aware of the specific sources of their power with patients and hence do not apply it optimally. After analyzing a large body of empirical research on the effects of social influence, French and Raven[15] differentiated five specific types of social power. Their analysis was based on the psychological changes induced through the relationship between the influencer and the object. The stronger the base of the power, that is the more important the relationship, the more power is exerted.

The first type of power distinguished by French and Raven is *reward power*. This depends on the ability to provide symbolic or material rewards—giving people what they want or need. In a physician-patient interaction, this would include approval, attention, time, or advice. It can also mean responding favorably to requests for medication, tests, procedures, or providing relief from pain or anxiety.

Coercive power depends on the ability to respond to a person's behavior in a punitive way, to create a negative or uncomfortable experience. Coercive power enables a person to force someone to act in a particular way or face a costly consequence. Coercive power is efficient in a situation where one has a captive audience, but it is costly in terms of relationship quality. Behavior that changes in response to coercion will revert back to its natural form when supervision is removed. Physicians are probably attributed a great deal of coercive power by patients. It is omnipresent in the physician's potential for giving disapproval, denying requests, prescribing aversive protocols, undesired diets, refusing to see the patient or answer phone calls, and withholding permission for desired activities. The ineffectiveness of coercive power, in the absence of supervision, may well account for the dismal rate of patient compliance with medication regimens, especially when they are dissatisfied with their relationships with their physicians.[21-23]

Legitimate power derives from people's perceptions that someone has an institutionalized right to exert influence on them. This type of power is definitely attributed to the physician by a patient through the act of initiating a consultation. Since payment for service is also a part of the contract, the legitimacy of the physician's power over the patient is confirmed. By contracting to pay for advice given, the patient acknowledges the legitimacy of the physician's right to give instructions. This right, in fact, becomes an obligation that the patient has instigated.

The more legitimate the power is perceived to be, the less resistance there is to the influence exerted. It must be understood that the legitimacy derives from internalized values, where the patient accepts the physician as a valid authority with a right to prescribe standards. If the patient has ambivalent feelings toward authority growing out of a history of conflicts with coercive or overdemanding authority figures (father, teachers, bosses), there may well be a tendency to thwart the authority of the physician. Many patients do have some problems with authority, so compliance is not always assured, regardless of the legitimacy of the power. In subsequent chapters, we will discuss ways in which the physician can avoid power struggles smoothly.

Referent power has to do with the person's desire to identify with the other. The desire to identify is heightened by the attractiveness of the source of influence. There is a clear parallel here with the affective parameter as outlined by Kelman[20] above. In terms of maintaining influence independent of observation by the power source, changes induced through referent power generally become independent quite rapidly. People want to be the way the role model, mentor, hero, or rescuer would want them to be. They want to do what is required. It makes them feel good. This implies that compliance can be assured in the outpatient setting. The patient wants to please the physician. The internalization mechanism causes the patient to feel competent and good when following directions. When thinking of "my doctor," the patient's self-esteem is raised by the perception of the relationship. The mechanism is not one of internalizing the values, but of a feeling of oneness or a desire for such an identity. It is part of the feeling of connectedness or belonging, which we discussed in the previous chapter. "My doctor says I'm OK" or, "My doctor says I'm doing well," really makes them feel good.

The last type of power outlined by French and Raven[15] is *expert power*. Unquestionably, patients accept the physician as an expert in medical matters and are therefore most vulnerable to being influenced.

The physician's word on psychological or social matters will also rarely be questioned. The less sure people are about an issue, the more open they are to being swayed by others' opinions. The more under stress a person feels, the more open that person is to help and suggestion. The more difficult the matter is to understand, the more persuasive the arguments of an expert are found to be. The type of change induced through acceptance of information from an expert power source becomes totally independent of that source and is absorbed into the cognitive structure of the person. French and Raven point out the interesting "sleeper effect" that occurs when information is at first not accepted by subjects because the source has a negative referent power connotation (an expert perhaps, but not liked or wanted to be identified with). Later, one finds that the subjects have been influenced after all. In political campaigns, distorted, unfavorable allegations about candidates are often accepted even by supporters, because they have been repeatedly heard and the facts have been separated from their source. The information later becomes part of the cognitive structure, the belief system, of the subject. Many studies have shown that subjects forget the source of a communication faster than the content, hence, the power of rumors.

Physicians have tremendous potential for correcting erroneous information concerning psychological issues that have been internalized by patients. Perhaps a hated authority figure has convinced a patient that he or she is not important as a person. This erroneous information results in poor self-esteem, a sense of helplessness, and a world view devoid of reinforcing experience. The physician's expressed interest in the patient is incongruent with the patient's own view of not counting at all. Since the physician is generally seen as a source of social power, the therapeutic effect of intentionally made supportive statements cannot be minimized. Conversely, physicians have the power to undermine patients' self-esteem and self-confidence. By talking down to the patient or discounting the patient's concerns, the physician reinforces the patient's low self-opinion. How particular evaluations or instructions are communicated becomes critical. For example, if a patient is concerned about a particular symptom such as a vague pain, the physician's offhand instruction, "Don't worry about it," not only discounts the patient but becomes an order that the patient cannot follow. This lowers self-esteem and exacerbates anxiety. However, if the physician says, "I have examined you and *I* see no cause for concern," or, "I'm not worried," then the patient can infer that the condition is truly benign. The statement on the part of the physician regarding the physician's concern taps into feelings of identification. The patient feels, "OK, my doctor is not worried, therefore I don't have to worry either," or, "My doctor is an expert on the matters. The doctor says it will go away by itself, so it can't be serious. I won't worry."

Some Final Words on Power

This has been a long and detailed section. The ability to manipulate others affords a measure of power and control that some physicians find uncomfortable. In writing about mental health professionals, Cone[24] points out that although some clinicians may have some conflicts regarding issues of power and control, they appear to be unaware that they already hold a powerful upper hand in relationship to their clients. Since this power already exists, Cone suggests that random, noncontingent, "unknowing" use has to be more frightening than the intentional application of the power in the service of the patient. This is precisely our point. We have tried to point out the rich sources of power inherent in the doctor-patient relationship. It is a given. Our purpose is to make the physician aware so that this power can be applied judiciously and skillfully toward the end of making the patient feel better.

BUILDING ON EXISTING SKILLS

Every physician who knows how to talk with and listen to patients has the basic tools with which to provide specific psychological support. Essential skills in the medical interview consist of establishing rapport, eliciting information, clarifying the patient's problems, and then communicating the diagnosis and management plan. Talking with patients is primarily a theme-centered conversation, a conversation focused on the patient's concerns.

Physicians are perhaps most skilled in the data collection aspect of the interview. In this connection, we propose that the types of questions to be asked in dealing with the psychological aspect of the patient's problems be designed to help the *patient* become aware of the affective state being experienced. This includes an awareness of current stresses, the reaction to them, major concerns, and options available for dealing with the stress. It also includes an assessment of what would be required to potentiate the initiation of action on the part of the patient, if appropriate, to reach some resolution. In this connection, we want to point out that this is *not* a psychiatric interview. We do not advocate a diagnostic workup or an in-depth analysis of the patient's coping mechanisms. We are not interested in deriving a categorical differential diagnosis of mental disease. Instead, we assume that the patient is distressed and propose that the process of inquiry be structured so as to give the patient the opportunity to reassess the situation in a more productive way. We are looking to normalize the patient's reaction. With this in mind, the data collection phase of the interview is specifically goal oriented, utilizing previously learned skills.

When physicians gather data, they usually approach the patient in a logically organized way: "What is troubling you?" "When did it start?" "What did you notice first?" "Describe the symptoms." "What makes it better?" Information is gathered, prioritized and synthesized. The physician attempts to get a comprehensive view, to avoid premature closure and then to diagnose the problem. Having done this, the doctor explains the findings, communicates the management plan, and reassures the patient. These communication skills are all that is required for adequately treating the psychological aspects of the patient's problems. What is involved is simply a conscious, focused, deliberate application of the therapeutic agent: *the physician*. This is accomplished through the medium of therapeutic talk. Talk that helps the patient to identify problems, recognize when they started, how they feel, and what is required to fix them. The quality of the interaction between the doctor and the patient promotes a positive effect on the patient's self-image and/or view of the world.

Communicating a Caring Attitude

The relationship between a *person* and the *other*, is essentially the most powerful therapeutic tool there is. How we relate to the other, the quality of the time we spend, is often communicated more clearly in the nonverbal than the verbal parts of the interaction. Physicians are aware of the value of eye contact, the powerful messages carried by body language, and the positive effect of nonjudgmental listening techniques. It is the quality of the time given the patient that determines the therapeutic effect, not the absolute amount of time that the physician spends. Does the physician pay attention? Show interest? Concentrate?

Every well-trained doctor should have these skills. These techniques have generally been *overlearned*, become automatic, having been performed over and over again. What is important regarding psychological support, as stated earlier, is to organize the data collection to be highly efficient, with the intent of clarifying the problem for the patient. It is the patient who needs to understand in order to have power. It is not useful for the physician to probe for details about how the situation evolved. It may satisfy the physician's curiosity, but is not therapeutic. It is not important to gather information about matters over which the physician can exert no control. However, it is extremely useful for the patient to gain awareness about the response that is generated by the situation and to recognize the legitimacy of that response. Applying the formula *person plus stress yields reaction*, the physician focuses on the reaction (which may well be the patient's presenting problem). In this case, reassurance consists of acknowledging to the patient that the symptoms, including the emergent emotional state, are appropriate. Patients then do not have to be upset about being upset or angry about being angry. They do not have to worry about being worried or depressed about being depressed. The physician has diagnosed the situation as being a stressor and pronounced the patient's reaction as a logical response given the patient's view. This is experienced as being highly supportive.

The attention that the physician gives the patient and the serious consideration given the patient's problems has an added therapeutic effect. The healing is in the relationship. The positive regard for the patient expressed by the physician's focusing attention on the psychosocial aspect of the patient's problems cannot be too highly emphasized. For most of us, attention from significant others is interpreted as a confirmation of our sense of worth and belonging. Children will do almost anything to get attention. We all know that if a child cannot get attention through some positive action, it can be expected that the child will act in some provocative fashion. Even a reprimand or a slap is better than no attention at all. It seems that there is a driving need to be attended to, even in negative ways. We need to feel connected to others, to be seen and responded to. By responding to the psychological needs of the patient in a positive and deliberate way, the physician enhances the patient's sense of worth. By focusing the patient on potential solutions to the problem or at least legitimizing the patient's reaction, the physician is enhancing the patient's sense of autonomy and competence.

Perhaps there are those who will still question the physician's qualifications for doing therapy. The simplest answer is that the opportunity is there. Patients may often not be aware of the specifics of what made them feel better. They only know that they feel bad enough to consult a physician and feel better after the visit.

DETERMINING THE CONTEXT OF THE VISIT

Probably the most important question that any practitioner asks about a patient's visit (other than an acute, life-threatening episode) is "Why is the patient coming now?" Mr. Jones has had a sore throat for two weeks. He denies any fever. He has no cough or other symptoms. His throat is slightly erythematous. What made him decide to come today? He does not seem to be that sick. It would seem that he felt at least this bad for the past two weeks. So why now? The best way to find out what Mr. Jones is most concerned about is to ask, "What are you afraid is going on?" It is also important to get some idea of what is happening in his life. What stress level is he dealing with? How well are his coping mechanisms working? Does he have adequate social supports? Information about his symptoms in the absence of the context of his current life situation is almost meaningless. The greatest danger lies in getting caught up in the details of Mr. Jones's experience. Many physicians are reluctant to explore the psychosocial aspects of a patient's problem because of the potential time-consuming nature of this process. Patients, when encouraged to talk, often consume great amounts of the physician's time without coming to any resolution. The physician feels battle weary and behind schedule without the satisfaction of having successfully treated anything specific.

The problem to be solved concerns eliciting background information quickly and efficiently and not having the patient feel cut off. We have devised a simple protocol for the exploration of the psychosocial context, which has specific goals. These limited goals include:

1. To raise the patient's awareness of the concomitant events that might be affecting his or her health status.
2. To focus the patient on the emotional state that is being experienced.
3. To guide the patient into specifying one aspect of the problem that is most troubling.
4. To focus on the manner in which the patient is handling the experienced stress.

5. **To provide an empathetic response, which makes the patient feel validated.**

We ask four basic questions. What is going on? How do you feel about it? What troubles you the most? How are you handling it? Then we give the patient a response showing we have understood that there is a problem and that the patient is handling it just as well as can be expected under the circumstances. It is crucial that the physician give this type of empathetic response. We have earlier pointed out how no response or an abrupt change of topic leaves the patient feeling dissatisfied, even when there was an opportunity to ventilate about a problem. When the patient expresses concerns about some issue, the physician *must* respond (if the physician wishes to be therapeutic). The phrase, "That must be very difficult for you," is extremely useful. We suggest that any time a physician is at a loss for words after being presented with some complicated or painful problem, the automatic reply, "That must be very difficult (or hard, or painful, or tiring, or discouraging) for you," is always appropriate. When it comes from a powerful, attractive, knowledgeable source such as the physician, such a response makes the patient feel much better.

Although the situation is tough, at least the response is reasonable. If the situation is truly difficult, as understood by the doctor, the patient feels much better and less subjectively out of control. Perhaps he or she is not as incompetent, worthless, or helpless as had been imagined. And perhaps it is not true that nobody cares, since the doctor obviously cares. Hope is rekindled and the patient is no longer demoralized. Tolerance for symptoms will be enhanced and the healing capacity of the body will be facilitated.[25,26]

Often patients will wish to go into great detail about their situations. The physician can interject that it is obvious that the situation is difficult but that under the circumstances the patient is doing well. Also, by paraphrasing the patient's concern and reactions to the problem, the physician indicates that there has been careful listening and that the patient has been understood. These well-learned techniques constitute the essence of psychological support.

A CLINICAL EXAMPLE

A 24-year-old woman visited the office complaining of a sore throat and a mild earache that she had had for 10 days. The chart showed that there had been several previous visits for minor complaints and some evidence of mild postpartum depression. Her youngest child was presently 12 months old. There were two older children in the home. Questioning by the physician elicited no particular acute stress, just a general lack of enthusiasm. Asked about the progress of the baby, the patient brightened somewhat. The physician then suggested that taking care of an active one-year-old, especially at this time of the year, when she wasn't feeling well herself, must be very difficult. The patient gave a deep sigh. "Oh, how I wish that there was someone to take care of me." "I can understand that," said the physician. He put his hand on her shoulder and guided her to the exam table. She smiled and relaxed.

We are not implying here that this simple interaction solved the patient's problems or cured her mild depression. We only suggest that as a result of the interaction the patient obviously felt better, as shown by her affect. We assume that she interpreted the physician's comments as indicating that her response to her problems was reasonable and that, therefore, she was seen as a reasonable person. This lifted her spirits and self-esteem.

SUMMARY

To provide comprehensive and personal medical care for patients, psychological as well as physical symptoms must be addressed. Many patients already consider their physician to be their primary source of mental health care. The true healing skills are those of communication and caring. Primary care physicians who establish relationships of trust, continuity, and nurturance with their patients already have a base for practicing psychotherapy.

Social power is defined as the potential to change the beliefs, attitudes, or behavior of another person. Physicians have both manifest (demonstrated) and attributed (assumed) power. Since physicians are powerful, attractive, and credible sources of information, they have the potential to influence patients' behavior and effect permanent attitude change. Social power can be divided into five types: reward, coercive, legitimate, referrent, and expert. Since all of these are both manifest and attributed to the physician, the opportunity exists to use this power base with the intent of making patients feel better.

Physicians already have the necessary interviewing skills, such as data collection, organization, information synthesis, and communication, that can be used to establish quality relationships demonstrating interest and attention. Simply by establishing the context of the patient's visit and providing an empathic response, the physician can help mitigate the patient's distress.

REFERENCES

1. France, R. D., Weddington, W. W., Jr., and Houpt, J. L. Referral of patients from primary care physicians to a community mental health center. *The Journal of Nervous and Mental Disease*, 1978, *166*, 594-598.
2. Lee, S. H., Gianturco, D. T., and Eisdorfer, C. Community mental health center accessibility. *Archives of General Psychiatry*, 1974, *31*, 335-339.
3. Locke, B. Z. and Gradner, E. P. Psychiatric disorders among the patients of general practitioners and internists. *Public Health Reports*, 1969, *84*, 167-173.
4. Brodaty, H. and Andrews, G. Brief psychotherapy in family practice: A controlled prospective intervention trial. *British Journal of Psychiatry*, 1983, *143*, 11-19.
5. McLean, P. D. and Miles, J. E. Training family physicians in psychosocial care: An analysis of a program failure. *Journal of Medical Education*, 1975, *50*, 900-902.
6. Stepansky, P.E. and Stepansky, W. Training primary physicians as psychotherapists. *Comprehensive Psychiatry*, 1974, *15*, 141-151.
7. Pierloot, R. A. The treatment of psychosomatic disorders by the general practitioner. *International Journal of Psychiatry in Medicine*, 1977-78, *8*, 43-51.
8. Pincus, H. A., Strain, J. J., Houpt, J. L., and Gise, L. H. Models of mental health training in primary care. *Journal of the American Medical Association*, 1983, *249*, 3065-3068.
9. Schwab, J. J. Depression in patients of internists. *Journal of Psychiatric Treatment and Evaluation*. 1983, *5*, 429-437.
10. Cousins, N. *The Healing Heart: Antidotes to Panic and Helplessness.* New York: Norton, 1983.
11. Benjamin, W. W. Sounding board: Healing by the fundamentals. *New England Journal of Medicine*, 1984, *311*, 595-597.
12. Ibid, p. 596.
13. Edelstein, L. The Hippocratic oath: Text, translation and interpretation. *Supplements to the Bulletin of the History of Medicine*, no. 1. Baltimore: Johns Hopkins Press, 1943.
14. McWhinney, I. R. *An Introduction to Family Medicine.* New York: Oxford University Press, 1981.
15. French, J. P. R. Jr., and Raven, B. H. The bases of social power. In Cartwright D. and Zander, A., eds., *Group Dynamics: Research and Theory*, 3rd ed. New York: Harper & Row, 1968.
16. Homans, G. C. *Social Behavior: Its Elementary Form.* New York: Harcourt Brace, 1961.
17. Collins, B. E. and Raven, B. H. Group structure: Attraction, coalitions, communication and power. In Lindzey, G. and Aronson, E., eds., *The Handbook of Social Psychology.* Reading, MA: Addison-Wesley, 1969.

18. Postman, N. *The Disappearance of Childhood*. New York: Delacorte, 1982.

19. Bacon, F. *Meditationes Sacrae*. Cited in Bartlett, J., *Familiar Quotations*, 13th ed. Boston: Little, Brown, 1955, p. 118.

20. Kelman, H. C. Compliance, identification and internalization: Three processes of attitude change. *Journal of Conflict Resolution*, 1958, *2*, 51-60.

21. Ley, P. The psychology of compliance. In Osborne, D. J. Gruneberg, M. M. and Eiser, J. R., eds., *Research in Psychology and Medicine*, Vol. 2. London: Academic Press, 1979.

22. Dunbar, J. M. Assessment of medication compliance. In Haynes, R. B., Mattson, M. E., and Engebretson, T. O. eds., *Patient Compliance to Prescribed Antihypertensive Medication Regimens*. Bethesda, MD: National Institutes of Health (NIH81-2102), 1980.

23. Brody, D. S. An analysis of patient recall of their therapeutic regimens. *Journal of Chronic Diseases*, 1980, *33*, 57-63.

24. Cone, J. W. Formal models of ego development: A practitioner's response. In Datan, N. and Ginsberg, L. H., eds., *Life-Span Developmental Psychology: Normative Life Crises*. New York: Academic Press, 1975.

25. Cassel, J. The contribution of the social environment to host resistance. *American Journal of Epidemiology*, 1976, *104*, 107-123.

26. Cobb, S. Social support as moderator of life stress. *Psychosomatic Medicine*, 1976, *38*, 300-314.

4
Basic Principles and Strategies of Psychotherapeutic Change

In this chapter we would like to discuss the effective elements of psychotherapy, especially those that can be incorporated into primary care practice. As we have pointed out in earlier chapters, psychological factors predispose the patient to illness and affect recovery from illness, therefore, psychotherapy becomes a critical part of any medical treatment. Psychotherapy means the treatment of emotional, behavioral, personality, or psychiatric disorders, primarily by verbal or nonverbal communication with the patient, rather than, or in addition to, treatments utilizing chemical or physical measures. Psychotherapy consists of the things we say—and how we say them—that make the patient feel better. It is the interaction with the patient, the therapeutic talk, that has the healing or at least ameliorating effect on the patient's distress.

Different schools of psychiatry and psychology will claim that their particular method of therapy is primary in facilitating the kind of change in self-image, world view, emotional response, or overt behavior that is associated with successful outcome in psychotherapy. We maintain that there is more than one way to view an elephant or the world. When we speak about world view it is important to remember that patients make assumptions about the nature of the world based on their experiences of the world since early childhood. Much of this process is out of the level of awareness. However, they create a model or map that represents reality according to their subjective interpretation. This is their *assumptive world view*. We all have an assumptive world view. The more neurotic we are, the more distorted this world view is. According to Maslow,[1] neurotic persons are not only *relatively* inefficient but are *absolutely* inefficient, since they do not perceive the real world as accurately or efficiently as do healthy persons. Maslow says that "The neurotic person is not only emotionally sick—he is cognitively *wrong*."[2] Perhaps the simplest definition for psychotherapy is what we do to "fix" patients' maps of the world so that they can figure out the way to go to get what they want.

Research has overwhelmingly demonstrated the effectiveness of psychotherapy over placebo or no-treatment approaches, but there is little evidence that demonstrates the actual superiority of one type of therapy over another.[3-5] However, certain approaches seem to lend themselves more effectively to specific types of clinical situations, as will be discussed later.

We are only concerned with those therapeutic features that work, regardless of the brand name. Our strong impression is that the most effective techniques are *generic*. We are not concerned with why something works but in *how*. We are interested in the practical application. When we talk about strategies that work, it becomes obvious that we must specify our goals. What is it that we want to accomplish? We can then figure out how this can be done.

THE GOALS OF THERAPY

Most simply put, the goal of psychotherapy is to make the patient feel better, that is, to lower levels of distress and combat feelings of being overwhelmed. As pointed out in Chapter 2, when patients feel overwhelmed by the circumstances of their lives or their reaction to these circumstances, they will develop a wide range of somatic and psychological symptoms. The most common symptoms from which patients suffer are anxiety and depression.[3,6] These symptoms develop because of patients' interpretations of their situation, not because of the situation proper. The experience of these symptoms further compromises patients' coping ability. Patients go on *tilt*.

The goal of psychotherapy is to make the patient feel better so that the patient can function better. When we talk about feeling—as related to psychotherapy—we are talking about the emotional or mental state of the patient. Specifically, we are concerned about the patient's sense of self-esteem and perceived personal power to deal with the current situation. When we talk about the patient functioning better, we mean being able to cope more productively with the demands of the internal and external environments. We expect that this improved coping will help to restore the patient's equilibrium, resulting in greater feelings of competence and belonging. Basically, then, our therapeutic goal is to help patients regain their normal sense of competence and so that they feel able to handle and affect the course of their lives. We also aim to restore patients' sense of connectedness, their sense of being acceptable in the human community.

Once the patient feels better, we can expect that the patient will be able to function better. When we speak of functioning, we include interpersonal relations, job performance, and the ability to mobilize the body's defenses in response to existent or potential disease.[7] We also expect that the patient will sleep better, have a decent appetite, and maintain a reasonable flow of energy. We project that in contrast to the vicious cycle of demoralization, depression of spirit and compromized immune response leading to disease and further demoralization, the body's healthy defenses will be engaged, leading to an enhanced sense of competence and then an improved ability to resist disease.[8]

Often the psychotherapeutic intervention will cause patients to make positive changes in their assumptive world view. This altered way of thinking and behaving results in more satisfactory experiences, providing a natural reinforcement mechanism and instigating a benevolent circle.[9]

Supportive Therapy

Traditionally, a broad distinction has been made between supportive psychotherapy and explorative psychotherapy. Supportive therapy is concerned with restoring premorbid or optimal functioning, while explorative therapy is concerned with exploring personality patterns to understand the etiology of disorders. Techniques promoted by proponents of supportive therapy include abreaction (catharsis—giving patients a chance to talk about the problem), dependency (being there for the patient), exploration of symptomatology, encouragement of productive behavior, and efforts at resolution through clarification. Basically, all effective therapy is supportive.

Explorative Therapy

In explorative therapy there is no overt interest in the patient's action. The expressed interest is in understanding feelings as related to their etiology. Jerome Frank has pointed out that if we mean by cure that we can eradicate the cause of illness, the "features of the patient's illness that psychotherapy can cure directly would be those caused by stress-producing distortions in the patient's assumptive world. Since the patient is an open psychobiological system, correction of these distortions would inevitably be reflected in changes in the neurophysiology of the central nervous system."[10]

We cannot stress too strongly that insight or understanding by itself has *no* practical benefit. Watzlawitz, Weakland, and Fisch in the book, *Change: Principles of Problem Formation and Problem Resolution*,[11] make the following point:

> Everyday, not just clinical, experience shows not only that there can be change without insight, but that very few behavioral or social changes are accompanied, let alone preceded, by insight into the vicissitudes of their genesis. It may, for instance, be that the insomniac's difficulty has its roots in the past: his tired, nervous mother may habitually have yelled at him to sleep and to stop bothering her. But while this kind of discovery may provide a plausible and at times even very sophisticated *explanation* of a problem, it usually contributes nothing towards its *solution*.

In a brilliant footnote these authors argue as follows:

> Such empirical findings are not out of line with general considerations, if these are thought through to their logical conclusions. There are two possibilities: 1) The causal significance of the past is only a fascinating but inaccurate myth. In this case, the only question is the pragmatic one: How can desirable change of present behavior be most efficiently produced? 2) There *is* a causal relationship between the past and present behavior. But since past events are obviously unchangeable, either we are forced to abandon all hope that change is possible, or we must assume that—at least in some significant respects—the past has influence over the present only by way of a person's *present* interpretation of *past* experience. If so, then the significance of the past becomes a matter not of "truth" and "reality," but of looking at it here and now in one way rather than another. Consequently, there is no compelling reason to assign to the past primacy or causality in relation to the present, and this means that the reinterpretation of the past is simply one of many ways of possibly influencing present behavior. In this case, then, we are back at the only meaningful question, i.e., the

pragmatic one: How can desirable change of present behavior be produced most efficiently?[11]

In essence, it is clear to us that *why someone is doing anything is irrelevant*. What is important is to help them to *change it*. (In some cases, very intellectual types may feel that they must understand *why* before they can bring themselves to change—but in the final analysis it is their decision to make a change that is effective, not understanding *why* they behaved the way they did in the first place.)

FIVE ELEMENTS SHARED BY PSYCHOTHERAPEUTIC TECHNIQUES

We have suggested that it is important to specify the generic helpful elements of psychotherapy. The field of the therapies includes a wide variety of modalities and orientations. There is long-term, short-term, individual, group, and family therapy. In any of these modalities, the orientation could be psychoanalytic, gestalt, transactional, dynamic, reality oriented, behavioral, rational emotive, neurolinguistic, or eclectic, to mention only a few. Regardless of theoretical orientation, there are basic principles and strategies that are associated with the therapeutic change process.[12] These are the generic forces that we wish to engage in the therapeutic interaction.

The Expectation of Receiving Help

Common to all psychotherapeutic modalities is the initially induced expectation that the therapy will be helpful. Jerry Frank has repeatedly pointed out that patients seek therapy because they are feeling helpless, hopeless, and demoralized.[13,14] Most recently, he has defined the demoralization commonly experienced by patients as "a state of subjective incapacity plus distress. The patient suffers from a sense of failure, loss of self-esteem, feelings of hopelessness or helplessness and feelings of alienation or isolation. These are often accompanied by a sense of mental confusion, which the patient may express as a fear of insanity."[15] The expectation that help is imminent helps to lift the patient from the depth of demoralization.

The Therapeutic Relationship

The second general principle associated with all psychotherapeutic modalities is the client's or patient's participation in a therapeutic relationship. This relationship exists for the sole purpose of fostering the well-being of the patient. A contract (or understanding) is made in which another person agrees to engage with the patient in a manner that fosters the expression of feelings and concerns in an accepting atmosphere. This contract for caring and concern is the core of therapy. It is the nature of the relationship that determines the efficacy of the healing process, whether we are discussing the classical analyst who listens and occasionally interprets, the Rogerian therapist who gives nonjudgmental reflections to the client, or the reality therapist who expects the patient to honor commitments and make no excuses. Regardless of theoretical orientation, it is the connection—the special relationship with the practitioner who communicates that he or she understands the patient, takes the patient seriously, and is devoted to the patient's welfare—that is the *generic* healing component.

Obtaining an External Perspective

The third factor found in all psychotherapies is giving patients the opportunity to obtain an external perspective on their problems. By bringing their perceptions of their situation to a person not directly involved, patients are exposed to alternative interpretations, made aware of potential options, and learn something about how other people might react to a similar situation. The external perspective affords patients an opportunity to check their possibly inaccurate perceptions of reality. If the listener does not get upset when hearing about the outrageous situation that the patient describes, perhaps there is some hope after all.

Encouraging Corrective Experiences

All psychotherapeutic modalities encourage corrective experiences. The definition of the corrective experience may vary according to the theoretical orientation of the practitioner, but until insights are put into practice and in some way change how patients relate to themselves, their world, and the significant others in their world, there is no healing. With the physician as cheerleader, patients are always encouraged to think and behave in new ways that result in a sense of enhanced well-being. This is the essence of a corrective experience. Patients are encouraged to react to situations in less destructive ways. As has been pointed out, the benefits of this improved behavior include gaining greater satisfaction from their interactions with others, which then promotes further gains.

The Opportunity to Test Reality Repeatedly

The last principle common to all psychotherapies is the opportunity to test reality repeatedly. Most patients have a limited range of behavior in certain situations. Their judgments of others, including others' intentions, is often quite inaccurate. By bringing to the physician perceptions of what has occurred, by looking at what the choices and options were, and by checking out their possibly faulty assumptions, patients are able to get a more accurate view of personal patterns of behavior, strengths, and vulnerabilities. Emotional and behavioral limitations will be reexamined. Certain situations that may previously have been judged as unattainable—not on the map—may be experienced as possibilities. In the course of therapy, expectations of self and others generally become more reasonable, and hence more likely to be satisfied.

THE MAJOR CONTRIBUTIONS OF SPECIFIC PSYCHOTHERAPEUTIC MODALITIES

We have outlined the major generic therapeutic components common to all psychotherapeutic interventions. It may also be helpful to point out some of the major contributions of specific schools or modalities of therapy that have particular relevance for application in the primary care practice. There are clearly some things that work better than others, some techniques that are easier to learn than others, and some that lend themselves more comfortably to a therapeutic encounter within a fifteen minute framework.

In general, people are simpler than insight schools give them credit for, but more complex than behavioral models suggest. By simpler we mean that a limited number of supportive techniques are highly effective, and by complex, we imply that people's reactions are determined by a multitude of factors both in and out of awareness. There is especially a reciprocal influence between the person and the environment. Taking our usual pragmatic approach, we will look at some of the most simple, efficient, easily learned, and theoretically enlightening approaches that can be incorporated in our brand of applied psychotherapy. It is lovely not to be bound to specific loyalties but instead to the welfare of our patients and our professional self-image.

Carl Rogers' Client-Centered Therapy

From Carl Rogers we have learned the value of relating to patients in a nonpossessive, accepting way, expressing our caring by providing accurate empathy.[16] The accepting physician creates an environment that facilitates the exploration of various possibilities for change. There is no therapeutic change without empathy and understanding.

Rogers taught the value of active listening. Empathetic understanding is communicated to the patient through techniques of paraphrasing, reflecting feelings, and making appropriate personal responses. The physician gives the patient permission to have and to express personal feelings and experiences. However, Rogers emphasizes that techniques are relatively unimportant except as a channel for providing the communication of positive regard and sensitive empathy. Smith[17] points out that very few psychotherapists identify themselves as pure Rogerians, but that Rogers "heads by far the list of those who have the greatest influence on counseling and psychotherapy. We surmise that Rogers' relationship emphasis permeates all current approaches to therapy." The skills of listening empathetically, paraphrasing, and summarizing accurately are essential in the fifteen minute hour.

Behavior Therapy

Perhaps the most important contribution of behavior therapy is conceptualizing psychotherapy as a learning process. For the behaviorist, psychotherapy rests on the assumption that human behavior is modifiable through psychological procedures.[18] Behavioral therapy has come a long way since Dollard and Miller[19] first developed their schema for understanding anxiety from a behavioral aspect. Behaviorists then started developing counterconditioning techniques to mitigate anxiety and have since created a whole armamentarium of techniques to modify patients' reactions to specific situations. Relaxation, desensitization, visualization, assertiveness training, and biofeedback all stem from behaviorism in that patients practice and learn new ways to manage themselves, their anxiety, and their behavior. Behaviorists have also determined that thinking is a behavior that can be modified and that modes of thinking affect the origin, maintenance, and change process related to various human problems.[20,21]

People are often not aware that how they think about a situation directly influences how they feel about it. The language used in thinking and speaking also directly affects the way we react to particular situations. Before we specifically look at modifications that can be made through cognitive restructuring and adjustments in word usage, let us quickly review one interesting way to understand and manage anxiety.

Models of Anxiety

Dollard and Miller's[19] formulation, first published in 1950, is still relevant, though rarely familiar to physicians. What Dollard and Miller suggested is that there are basically three models of anxiety, that is, three prototypes of situations that precipitate feelings that people experience as anxiety: approach-approach, avoidance-avoidance, and approach-avoidance on the same pole.

In the approach-approach condition, a patient has two desires or options that are available, and a choice must be made. As the patient gets closer to one, the other gets further away. Since the patient wants both, anxiety is generated. Sometimes these are specific situations such as choosing between security or more pay, a vacation or a new car; often the definition of self is involved in maintaining a desirable self-image such as the good mother versus the effective business woman (role strain).

+ ---- Patient ---- +

Mrs. Jones comes to the office complaining of a pinched nerve in her neck. She has had trouble sleeping and is really in pain. After inquiring into what is presently going on in her life, we find that she has been offered a wonderful job in a travel agency, but that she really wants to be home for her husband and children. Now that her neck has gone out of whack, she no longer has to make a decision. In an approach-approach conflict, pointing out the dynamics in the situation and the fact that either way the outcome is positive, as the patient will get something she wants, is often enough to reduce the anxiety.

In the avoidance-avoidance condition, the patient is caught between two negative situations. Both situations arouse fear or other unpleasant emotions; as the patient runs from one negative pole, the other gets closer. This generates high levels of anxiety and usually will immobilize the patient at dead center.

$$- \quad ---- \quad \text{Patient} \quad ---- \quad -$$

Mr. Brown hates his job. He has to drag himself to work every morning. He is thinking about quitting his job, but there is high unemployment in his town and every time he thinks about his financial situation his ulcer kicks up. He is also doing a good job of beating himself up for not being able to make a decision. Often just giving the patient permission to be there at dead center is therapeutic. Other effective techniques include desensitization through relaxation, providing support (evoking a positive response coupled with the negative stimulus), or helping the patient see the situation in a different light. Perhaps Mr. Brown can make some changes in his job, plan to start a business in town, or think about moving to a more desirable area. Even knowing that there are other choices and then making a decision to stay can be very therapeutic. Any of these techniques will reduce the perceived negativity of the pole.

Perhaps the most interesting model is approach-avoidance on the same pole. This situation is extremely common. It occurs when someone is attracted to a situation that also arouses fear.

Charles has met a woman he really admires. He wants to get close to her but at the same time he is afraid of intimacy. When he is not with her, her desirability is very strong; as he gets closer, his fear becomes overpowering. Anxiety at the inability to get what he wants becomes crippling. Charles moves back and forth, never really making contact, never really going away. He has all kinds of somatic complaints, and every time his friend gets close, he picks a fight with her about something, perhaps her lack of sympathy for his suffering. It has been our experience that both physician and patient gain from understanding and identifying this model. It is very useful. It creates an "ah-ha!" reaction that somehow makes the situation easier to bear. Then the patient can decide whether or not to hang in there with the fear in order to get what he wants.

The ABCs of Behavior

According to behaviorists, all behavior has an *antecedent* condition, the *behavior* occurs, and then there is a *consequence*. If the consequence is rewarding (reinforcing) to the person, we can expect that the behavior is more likely to recur. If the consequence is not reinforcing, the behavior is less likely to recur. In trying to modify behavior, the physician can suggest making changes in the prebehavior situation—those antecedent cues that trigger the behavior. "Do not have fattening foods in the house." "Do not argue with husbands when they have been drinking." "Do not take kids shopping when they are tired." Or the modification can be made in the consequences of the behavior. "Do not give in to children when they whine." "Give children attention when they are being helpful, quiet, responsible, etc." "Reward any desirable behavior and ignore bad behavior." More will be said about this in Chapter 8.

Reinforcements are most effective when they follow immediately after the desired behavior. When attempting to teach a new behavior, rewards can first be given for behavior that is closer to the goal than is usually the case (shaping behavior), and then gradually only the successful outcomes are rewarded. To teach something new or form a new habit, every successful attempt must be rewarded. To maintain behavior, once it is learned, *variable schedules of reinforcement*, which provide rewards once in a while and with no predictable pattern, are most effective, as witnessed by the continuing fascination of people with one-armed bandits in Las Vegas and Atlantic City.

Behavior that is not reinforced will *extinguish*, meaning that it will cease to occur. Unfortunately, this is a gradual process with predictable relapses and is easily sabotaged by an occasional *reinforcement*. In promoting new behavior in our patients, we have devised a scoring system based on integrating this understanding. More will be said about this in Chapter 7.

Cognitive Therapy

Albert Ellis[22] introduced rational emotive therapy (RET) in 1956, claiming that people do not react directly, emotionally, or behaviorally to the events they encounter in their lives, rather that people cause their own reactions by the way they interpret or evaluate the events they experience. These evaluations, according to Ellis, are based on a set of *irrational* beliefs. Ellis has a different set of ABCs. The activating event (A) does not directly cause (C), the emotional and behavioral response; our beliefs (B) about (A) do. Ellis distinguishes between situations that are unfortunate, sad, inconvenient, undesired, etc. and the usual interpretations that things are awful, terrible, hopeless, should be different, etc.

Ellis suggests that we need to examine the "musts" or "shoulds" in our lives. In this characteristic fashion he puts them into three categories:

1. Musturbatory ideology I says that we *must* do well and gain approval at *all* times or else we are rotten people. We *must* have sincere love and respect from all people we consider significant. Other people *must* be able to rely on us, there *must* be a high order of certainty in the universe, and we *must* be able to trust authority figures implicitly or else we cannot feel OK.
2. Musturbatory ideology II says that people *must* treat us considerately and kindly, just as we wish to be treated, or they *should* be punished by society or the universe.
3. Musturbatory ideology III concerns itself with conditions under which we live that *should* be how we want them to be and the fact that we get ourselves upset when we become aware that they are not as we wish them to be.

Ellis asserts that all of these conditions are desirable, but to believe that they are necessary for survival or even happiness is *irrational*. Therefore, he suggests a strategy that attacks the beliefs and through debating, discriminating, defining, counters the inappropriate response and elicits a healthier consequence. Patients are given tasks to write arguments against their irrational assumptions. Beck[21] used these techniques very successfully to help severely depressed persons counter the negative thoughts and evaluations of self, others, and circumstances that trigger and maintain depressive syndromes. These techniques are powerful, especially when promoted by a physician. We have simplified and incorporated them, as will be seen in Chapter 8.

The Role of Language in Therapy

In the *Structure of Magic*,[23] Bandler and Grinder did not intend to create a new school of psychotherapy, although neurolinguistic programming (NLP) directly resulted from this work. These authors, who define themselves as *linguists*, simply tried to make understandable and teachable the language skills used by some of the world's most talented therapists. Starting with the basic premise that there is an irreducible difference between the actual world and our experience of it, that each of us creates a representation of the world that then governs our behavior, and that since no two people have the same experience, we all have different models of the world, Bandler and Grinder examine the process by which these models are built.

First, all information about the world gets processed through our various senses, particularly the visual, auditory, and kinesthetic, and in order to process this information effectively, we tend to organize it in specific ways, sorting likes and creating categories. People seem to choose a predominant sense and will communicate this in the descriptive language they use. The visually oriented person will "see what you mean," the auditory dominant person will "hear you," while the kinesthetic will "feel" that they understand. In making interventions, it is useful to note and compliment the dominant sense of the patient. Bandler and Grinder found that the most successful therapists seem to respond automatically in the same mode as the patient, but this is a skill that can be learned.

Back to the map. There are primarily two groups of people, one that is able to respond creatively and cope productively with problems, and another that generally perceives few options, none of which is attractive. Bandler and Grinder suggest the difference lies in the fact that the second group has an impoverished map. How is it possible that these limited models, which causes them pain in the face of a multifaceted, rich, and complex world, are maintained? Well, there are three particular mechanisms that tend to block growth and the process of new experience: generalization, deletion, and distortion.

Generalization is an ability necessary for organizing information and coping with the world. *Generalizing* from the experience of being burned that touching a hot stove is not a good idea has survival value, but generalizing that stoves are dangerous and must be avoided is a limiting view. Generalizing that it is bad to express any feelings because one was discouraged from expressing negative feelings as a child may generalize to feelings being bad, period.

Based on early generalizations, people *delete*, that is selectively filter out, experience that counters the established view they have acquired. For example, people block themselves from hearing messages of caring that conflict with generalizations made about their self-worth. People who think of themselves as stupid will not hear being told that they are smart; on the contrary, they will think that the other person must really think they are awfully stupid to expect them to believe such nonsense. Hence, we insist on saying, "Wow, that was a difficult problem," instead of, "Gee, you did that well."

The third modeling process involves *distorting* sensory data to conform to preexisting notions. People hear and see what they expect to hear and see. Given a variety of experience, people will notice only those aspects that confirm their sense of themselves and the universe.

Language is used to organize what is happening in the world and how the patient feels about it. It affects how the patient represents past experiences in the present, to include rules about what behaviors are acceptable, how present experience is organized, what is in awareness, and the way the patient organizes future experiences and expectations regarding the outcome of behavior. Language is the medium for making corrections in the world view.

The process of therapy aims to challenge the generalizations, deletions, and distortions inherent in the patients' experience of reality and thereby to introduce changes into their models of the world.

In challenging generalizations, absolutes, such as *always, never, everyone,* and *no one,* need to be questioned, for example: "You're *absolutely always* in pain?" "*No one* has *ever* accepted your ideas?" "You've *never* done *anything* right?"

Deletions are expressed through leaving gaps in expressions. In challenging deletions, it is useful to get patients to specify missing information. When a patient says, "I'm afraid," the physician must respond, "Of what, *specifically* are you afraid?" The response to "I'm not good enough" is "In what *way* are you not good, and for *what?*" Another possible challenge would be: "How good is good enough?"

Distortions often occur when patients change verbs into nouns such as "relating" to "relationship," or "deciding" into "decision." Bandler and Grinder point out that turning a process into an event, which is then seen as unchangeable, is limiting, guilt-producing, and destructive.

Patient: "I really regret my decision."
Response: "What stops you from changing your mind now?"

Patient: "My relationship is a disaster."
Response: "Is there a way you respond to your partner in a different way?"

In challenging models, the physician questions not only absolutes, but imposed limits (the can'ts, shoulds, musts, and impossibilities—"Why not?"), imposed values (the rights, wrongs, goods, and bads), and in general helps the patient to create a richer representation of possibilities.

Reality Therapy

Perhaps the approach to psychotherapy that most resembles ours, at least as far as the therapeutic relationship is concerned, is reality therapy. Psychiatrists might see a patient as mentally ill, a cognitive therapist might feel the patient has irrational beliefs. Maslow says the patient is inefficient, but William Glasser[24] contends that patients are *irresponsible*, meaning that they do not take responsibility for their behavior. Glasser suggests that certain people are unsuccessful in finding a relevant identity for themselves in our role-oriented society and when they fail, they cope by developing symptoms or irresponsible behavior that causes them and those around them much suffering. Glasser sees the physician's role as becoming *involved* and helping these unfortunates to develop and maintain a successful identity and function more effectively.

The essence of reality therapy is establishing a warm and understanding relationship, helping the patient accept the interest shown, breaking patterns of loneliness and self-defeat. The patient is encouraged to go out into the world and make changes, act more responsibly, become aware of and evaluate current behavior, and make realistic plans and firm commitments to the physician for carrying them out. No excuses are accepted. If a plan was reasonable, there are no excuses. There is also no punishment. The physician simply insists that the commitment be honored. Patients become aware that there are consequences in real life for failure to carry out commitments. However, the therapeutic relationship remains one of respect, caring, and involvement through the setting of reasonable expectations and monitoring of results. It really works.

Psychoanalytically Oriented Psychotherapies

The unique contribution of psychodynamic theories comes from pointing out the hidden agendas that pervade interpersonal relationships and the effect of maladaptive personal responses that are influenced by past experiences and projected onto current relationships. The way patients define themselves as loving, hateful, or inadequate is an ongoing process. Some of this process is purely symbolic and unconscious, while some is within the awareness of the patient. Since much of this behavior is demonstrated in relation to the physician, an opportunity is created to bring these dynamics into focus. This phenomenon is usually referred to as *transference*, since the patient transfers the emotional reaction attached to significant authority figures (out of the past) onto the physician. The process of renaming and redefining then focuses on relabeling the underlying impulses, strivings, purposes, or attitudes.[12] These redefined tendencies should then be used to try to figure out what patients want *now* and to look for constructive ways for achieving these ends.

It is only when the patient applies the insight gained through the interaction with the physician to change behavior in relation to other significant people that one can say that the therapy has been successful. This is one of the reasons that the brief sessions are so powerful. We are much less concerned about the patient's behavior toward the physician than we are about patients' behavior in their everyday world. Patients will find that their emotional responses to previously upsetting or limiting situations will actually change. Their perception of reality becomes more accurate and they become aware of having more options.

FOUR MODELS OF HELPING AND COPING

Now that we have discussed some of the techniques that are productive in facilitating change, we would like to explore some of the underlying assumptions that are involved in the basic process of helping another person cope with various problems of living. Understanding these assumptions is useful, since particular models lend themselves more effectively to particular situations. Because this material is important and is generally unfamiliar to physicians, we will go into some detail.

In April 1982, an article in the *American Psychologist* distinguished four specific models of helping and coping. The authors, a group of social psychologists headed by Philip Brickman of the University of Michigan, determined that it was necessary to bridge the gap between the social psychology literature on helping behavior that experimentally studies helper characteristics and the clinical psychology literature that tries to determine the efficacy of outcome in specific helping relationships. They decided to focus on the way choices about giving material aid, instruction, exhortation, discipline, emotional support, or other forms of help are made. They were also interested in determining the consequences resulting from these choices.[25]

In looking at any problem, we assume that it is critical to arrive at an understanding of the cause of the situation. How did this happen? Who is to blame? Brickman and his colleagues suggest that, on the contrary, people are less concerned about understanding the causes of events than about controlling behavior, "both their own and other people's to maximize desired outcomes."[26]

In assigning moral responsibility for a problem, we must distinguish between blame and control. We assign blame to people we hold responsible for having created problems. We blame people who smoke two packs of cigarettes per day for 40 years for the COPD or lung cancer they develop. It is assumed that had they acted differently, the particular situation might not have evolved. We assign control to people when we acknowledge their ability to influence or change events. When talking about problems and solutions, we must distinguish between taking responsibility for creating problems that involves having control over past events (deserving blame) and for having responsibility for a solution that entails control over future events. Although clearly responsible (having had control) for creating a problem, we may not have the control over the resources required for achieving resolution. When we say "You made the trouble—you fix it," we unwittingly assume that finding out who is to blame for a problem is the same as finding a solution, which is decidedly not so! Also, finding out how a problem developed may help us prevent its recurrence, but at this time it does not potentiate achieving a solution.

By assigning responsibility or lack thereof for causing or solving problems, four fundamentally different orientations (models) of helping and coping are derived. The implications of these models to clinical practice cannot be too highly emphasized.

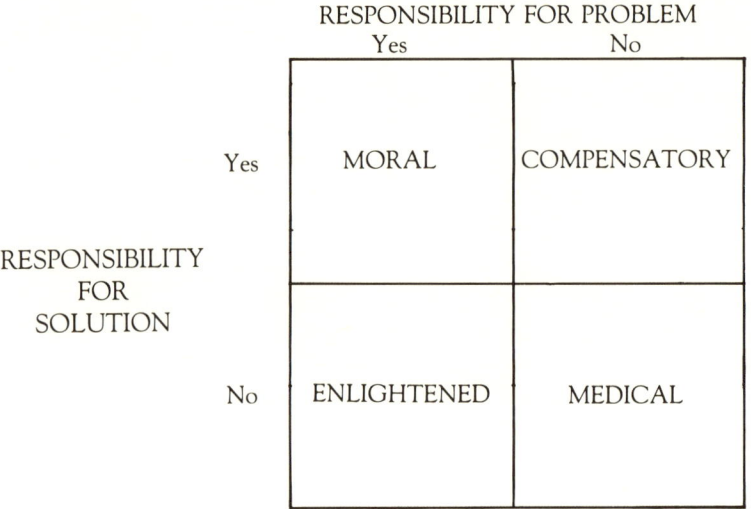

FIGURE 1. Four models of helping and coping. Adapted from Brickman et al. (1982)

The Moral Model

In the moral model, people are held responsible for both problems and solutions. When an individual applies this model, the assumption is that help from others is not needed. Individuals are seen as strong by nature and should exercise will power to solve whatever problems have been created. The value of this model is that it presents individuals with a sense of power over their lives. The danger is that it fosters a sense of omnipotence that must ultimately be shattered. Victims of inherited disorders or diseases like leukemia tend to believe that they are responsible for having chosen this situation. In the application of the moral model, the person is responsible for creating and effecting a solution and the role of the helper is simply to be a cheerleader and exhorter to action.

The Compensatory Model

In the compensatory model, people are not held responsible for having created problems; they are seen as having been handicapped or deprived. However, they are held responsible for effecting solutions through asking for and using the help that is available. Brickman and his colleagues contend, "The strength of the compensatory model for coping is that it allows people to direct their energies outward, working on trying to solve problems or transform their environment without berating themselves for their role in creating these problems, or permitting others to create them in the first place."[27]

The Medical Model

In the medical model, people are not held responsible for either the creation or solution of a problem. People are seen as sick and all that is required of them is acceptance of treatment by experts. Brickman and his colleagues see the practice of medicine only as a special case in a broader set of expectations about human behavior. In this model, human behavior is characterized as being controlled by forces outside the person that reward and punish. People are seen as weak and needing to be told exactly what to do. In this case, the helper prescribes a solution and the individual has responsibility only for following the orders of the expert. The major problem with this model is that it fosters dependency. If people feel that all their emotional or physical upsets are disorders that must be treated by professionals, the dependency fostered leads to subsequent psychological and physical deterioration.

The Enlightened Model

The final model shown has been named the enlightened model. In labeling this model, the authors suggest that people are seen as *needing* to be enlightened. They need to be explicitly made aware that they are responsible for having created their problems. They are guilty and need to be enlightened about their true nature. They have clearly demonstrated that they have gotten themselves into serious problems through their own failings. Now, they can only be helped by confessing their weakness and submitting to the stern discipline of the authoritarian helper, who will save them. The basic philosophy and success of AA (Alcoholics Anonymous) and various drug rehabilitation programs is based on the application of this model. When treating persons suffering addictive disorders, this may well be the treatment of choice, because it has been shown to work.

Application

Although Brickman and his colleagues argue that these models are mutually exclusive and internally consistent, we contend that the physician's assessment of whether the patient feels responsible (had control) for the creation and/or solution of a problem can determine the most effective therapeutic intervention. In all cases, we would be concerned with outcome rather than etiology. The question to ask is how we can present this situation to the patient in order to make the patient feel most competent to respond in a constructive way.

The patient's beliefs concerning personal responsibility rather than the actual circumstances of the situation determine the patient's reaction. Jerry Frank has pointed out that all psychiatric interventions can only alter a patient's interpretation of an event, not the actual situation.[9] In general, Rule 1 (see Chapter 9) is: Do not take responsibility for things that you cannot control. However, sometimes, taking responsibility for the problem (even if you didn't have control of all the circumstances), as in the case of some rape victims, helps to *decrease anxiety* (since it implies that it is not a totally random and uncontrollable world). This approach is not necessarily to be discouraged as long as the victim decides what steps to take to protect herself in the future (moral model). In other cases, if *guilt* is the major reaction, the physician can apply the compensatory model, making the victim aware of the lack of responsibility for the event and the subsequent need to learn ways to prevent recurrences. It is most important for the physician to determine the patient's orientation and start there. Moving the patient to a more appropriate model over time is the essence of therapy.

PUTTING IT INTO PRACTICE

Having outlined the elements of the therapeutic encounter and various potential models that are relevant in the helping relationship, we need to specify exactly how this gets translated into primary practice.

PLISSIT

Any encounter that inspires the patient's hopes for improvement, be it as a result of one visit or several, is therapeutic. However, it is useful for the primary care physician to have a protocol in mind for use for guiding the level of intervention.

A mechanistic, but practical and effective, hierachical system was first introduced by Annon[28] in the context of sex therapy. This four-step process is easily remembered and simple to apply.

In a potential therapeutic situation where the patient is concerned with certain reactions to a particular situation, the levels of intervention go from permission giving, to offering limited information, to specific suggestions, to a contract for intensive therapy.

P Stands for Permission

The patient is assured that the reaction that is being experienced is normal under the circumstances. This small intervention may alter the patient's assumptive world view. The patient recognizes that it is OK to be depressed and does not have to be depressed about being depressed. The patient may have lost his temper and yelled at his wife. The physician assures him it is OK to get angry, especially when one is under stress. Under the circumstances that can happen. The patient does need to let his wife know that he is sorry. It is important to give people permission to feel the way they feel, because if they could feel any other way at that particular time, they would. Regardless of the reaction, the physician's acceptance makes the patient feel more comfortable with the emotional state being experienced.

LI Stands for Limited Information

The patient is given information that explains the emotional state being experienced and helps provide realistic expectations for the patient and others. For example, the patient in a situation of crisis is told that in general, when people experience great amounts of stress, they react by feeling overwhelmed, confused, less capable of making decisions or solving problems, have trouble sleeping, etc. This normalization helps get the patient off *tilt*. The patient feels as though under the circumstances the reaction is appropriate after all. Information processing is a high-order coping skill, and by offering accurate and pertinent information, the physician is leading to the patient's strength.

SS Stands for Specific Suggestions

Specific suggestions can be given to the patient to examine options, talk to friends, get into a self-help organization, take time out, keep a journal, or any other specific strategy that helps to engage the patient's healthy functioning self and promote constructive coping behavior. The physician's interest and confidence that the patient is competent and in control helps to foster this behavior in the patient.

IT Stands for Intensive Therapy

Intensive therapy as it applies to the primary care setting suggests that the physician enters into an agreement to work with the patient over time. Appointments are scheduled and the physician contracts to offer support for the patient for a specific time to help to resolve a particular life problem. By engaging in a therapeutic contract with the patient, all five of the criteria specified in the section on essential psychotherapeutic elements are fulfilled. Positive expectations that help is forthcoming are instigated. A therapeutic relationship is established. An external perspective for the patient's problem becomes available. Corrective experiences are encouraged, and the patient is given the opportunity to test reality repeatedly. The physician agrees to be there to share in the process with the patient.

SUMMARY

Psychotherapy means the treatment of emotional, behavioral, personality, or psychiatric disorders, primarily through communication with the patient. Psychotherapy has been shown to be effective. The actual therapeutic features are generic to the process of making the patient feel better, that is, less overwhelmed.

Supportive therapy focuses on the patient's strength, while exploratory therapy aims to understand etiology of feelings. It is more important to help patients change their reactions than to understand their source. Common elements among psychotherapeutic techniques include: (1) the expectation of receiving help, (2) participation in a therapeutic relationship, (3) obtaining an external perspective on problems, (4) the encouragement of corrective experiences, and (5) the opportunity to test reality repeatedly.

In general, people are simpler than insight schools give them credit for, but more complex than behavioral models suggest. Carl Rogers's contribution relates to the value of accurate empathy and non-possessive caring in a therapeutic relationship. Behavior therapies underscore the importance of human learning in the process of modifying behavior. Anxiety presents in approach-approach, avoidance-avoidance, and approach-avoidance conflicts. All behavior has an antecedent condition and is followed by a consequence. In order to modify behavior, either the antecedent cues or the consequences can be changed. Reinforcements can be used to teach or maintain behavior. Behavior can be extinguished through nonreinforcement. Rational-emotive therapy is based on modifying irrational beliefs that affect how people react to situations. Language is used to record and classify our perceptual experience of the world. Through processes of generalization, deletion, and distortion, people build impoverished maps or models of the world, which then limit their perceived options. The therapeutic process challenges these generalizations, deletions and distortions in order to create a richer representation of possibilities. Reality therapy, through the creation of a warm and understanding relationship, encourages the patient to accept responsibility for becoming more effective. Psychoanalytically oriented therapies bring *transferred* emotional responses into focus and use the insight gained to precipitate change.

Strategies for helping and coping rest on assumptive models attributing responsibility for the cause of a problem and the responsibility for effecting a solution, based on having control of previous or current circumstances. In the *moral model*, people are held responsible both for causing and solving a problem. In the *compensatory model*, there is no blame for causing the problem, but responsibility for its solution. The *medical model* absolves the patient from both responsibility for causing or fixing a problem. The *enlightened model* assumes guilt on the part of the patient for causing the problem but inability to effect a solution. Application of the appropriate model can facilitate therapy.

In determining appropriate levels of therapy, the acronym, PLISSIT, connotes a hierarchy of interventions consisting of giving permission, offering limited information, making specific suggestions, and setting up a contract for intensive psychotherapy.

REFERENCES

1. Maslow, A. H. Self-actualizing people: A study of psychological health. *Personality*, 1950, Symposium 1, 11–34.
2. Ibid, p. 15.
3. Smith, N. L., Glass, G. V., and Miller, T. I. *Benefits of Psychotherapy*. Baltimore: Johns Hopkins University Press, 1980.
4. Shapiro, D. A. and Shapiro, D. Meta-analysis of comparative therapy outcome studies: A replication and refinement. *Psychological Bulletin*, 1982, *92*, 581–604.
5. Prioleau, L., Murdock, M., and Brody, N. An analysis of psychotherapy vs. placebo studies. *The Behavioral and Brain Sciences*, 1983, 6, 275–310.
6. Sloane, R. B., Staples, F. R., Cristol, A. H., Yorkston, N. J., and Whipple, K. *Psychotherapy Versus Behavior Therapy*. Cambridge, MA: Harvard University Press, 1975.
7. Hales, D. Mind over body: Old theories, new proof. *Medical World News*, October 10, 1983, 58–72.
8. Pelletier, K. R. *Mind as Healer: Mind as Slayer*. San Francisco: Delacorte, 1977.
9. Frank, J. D. Therapeutic components. In Myers, J. M., ed., *Cures by Psychotherapy: What Effects Change?* New York: Praeger, 1984.
10. Ibid., p. 17.
11. Watzlawitz, P., Weakland, J. H., and Fisch R. *Change: Principles of Problem Formation and Problem Resolution*. New York: Norton, 1974.
12. Goldfried, M. R. Rapprochment of psychotherapies. *Journal of Humanistic Psychology*. 1983, *23*, 97–107.
13. Frank, J. D. Psychotherapy: The restoration of morale. *American Journal of Psychiatry*, 1974, *131*, 271–274.
14. de Figueiredo, J. M. and Frank, J. D. Subjective incompetence, the clinical hallmark of demoralization. *Comprehensive Psychiatry*, 1982, 23, 253–363.
15. Frank, J. D. Therapeutic components, op. cit., p. 19.
16. Rogers, C. The neccessary and sufficient conditions of therapeutic personality change. *Journal of Consulting Psychology*, 1957, *21*, 95–103.
17. Smith, D. Trends in counseling and psychotherapy. *American Psychologist*, 1982, *37*, 802–809.
18. Bandura, A. Psychotherapy as a learning process. *Psychological Bulletin*, 1961, *58*, 143–59.
19. Dollard, J, and Miller, N. E. *Personality and Psychotherapy*. New York: McGraw-Hill, 1950.
20. Ellis, A. *A New Guide to Rational Living*. North Hollywood, CA: Wilshire Books, 1975.
21. Beck, A. T. *Cognitive Therapy and Emotional Disorders*. New York: New American Library, 1979.
22. Ellis, A. The basic clinical theory of rational-emotive therapy. In Ellis, A. and Grieger, R., *Handbook of Rational-Emotive Therapy*. New York: Springer, 1977.
23. Bandler, R. and Grinder, J. *The Structure of Magic I: A Book about Language and Therapy*. Palo Alto, CA: Science and Behavior Books, 1975.

24. Glasser, W. *Reality Therapy: A New Approach to Psychiatry.* New York: Harper & Row, 1965.
25. Brickman, P., Rabinowitz, V. C., Karuzaza, J. Jr., Coates, D., Cohn, E., and Kidder, L. Models of helping and coping, *American Psychologist,* 1982, 37, 368-384.
26. Ibid., p. 369.
27. Ibid., p. 372.
28. Annon, J. S. *Behavioral Treatment of Sexual Problems: Brief Therapy.* New York: Harper & Row, 1976.

5
Differences in Approach to Therapy Between the Primary Care Physician and the Psychiatrist

In this chapter we will explore some of the major differences in both process and outcome between therapeutic interventions that we propose can be made by the primary care physician and traditional treatment as provided by a psychiatrist or other mental health professional. We will explore these differences from several angles. First, we will look at patient expectations and reactions. Then we will examine certain aspects of the doctor-patient relationship. We will then specify our perception of the physician's investment in the patient's problems, and last, we will suggest some specific approaches that are available in primary care.

There is an old story about a secretary who went to work for a psychiatrist. After only a few short weeks, she resigned. When asked about why she quit the job, she reported to her friends, "I just couldn't win. He was always analyzing everything I did. If I got to work late, he said it was because I was hostile. When I got to work early, he wondered why I was anxious. Those days I got to work on time, he accused me of being compulsive." Psychiatrists deal with a selected sample of humanity and learn what they know about people through this interaction with their patients.[1] Psychiatrists (and other mental health professionals) are trained to look for pathology. After discovering psychopathology in a patient, the psychiatrist's task is to describe and classify the observed phenomena according to the appropriate DSM III[2] category and devise a coherent theoretical explanation for the etiology of the symptom. Although in psychiatry the process of making a diagnosis is considered to be part of the treatment,[1] often this activity provides no symptom relief for the patient. We feel that it is the task of the primary care physician to note and treat all psychological distress evident in patients regardless of other presenting problems.

THE ROLES OF THE PATIENT AND PHYSICIAN IN THE THERAPY PROCESS

One of the most widely accepted tenets of psychotherapy is that in order for the patient to benefit from treatment, the patient must ask for help and be open to receiving it. When a physician refers a patient to a mental health center or an individual psychiatric practitioner, there generally will be an acknowledgment of the appropriateness of the referral and then a request to have the patient call personally to set up the initial appointment for evaluation. It is accepted practice to consider the patient's taking action to seek help as the first positive step in the therapeutic process.

Patients may be reluctant to admit that they need psychiatric treatment. The idea of defining themselves as mental patients is an impediment to seeking help. Patients often do not follow through on referrals, even when they are made.[3] Studies show that somewhere between 15 and 75 percent of patients who are referred for psychotherapy fail to keep initial appointments.[4] In addition, 30 to 60 percent of psychiatric patients in outpatient clinics drop out after only two to five sessions.[5] The reported attrition rate for private psychiatrists is almost as high.[6] Although there is some evidence that even a single session of psychotherapy can be very effective, because of the ego-strengthening function that is implied in such brevity of treatment,[7] when patients are referred and it is not their idea, not only is the dropout rate high, but a study by Bowden and his colleagues[8] found that about half of the patients dropping out were feeling worse than when starting treatment. It is clear that referrals must be considered carefully.

Every employment application asks whether you have been treated for a mental or emotional disorder. Once treatment by a psychiatrist or other mental health professional has been obtained, patients have two choices: one is to lie about their medical history, and the other is to identify themselves as mental patients. Mental patients are often seen as people who have been or are suffering from a type of disorder that carries a social stigma. Who can forget the case of Senator Eagleton, whose candidacy for vice-president of the United States was hastily withdrawn when it became known that he had been treated for depression. It is not having been depressed that marks the unacceptable candidate, it is a record of having been diagnosed and treated for an affective disorder, a mental disease. Although in some social circles, comparing notes about what one's analyst has to say may be an accepted cocktail party sport, many middle- and lower-class patients are intimidated by the prospect of a psychiatric consultation.

Thomas Szasz[9] is probably the best known critic of psychiatric labeling, but others[10,11] have pointed out that psychiatric labeling can sometimes be used in pejorative ways as a form of social coercion. Certainly, when treatment is proposed before the patient has recognized the need, this can be initially deflating to the patient's already fragile sense of self-esteem. This loss of feelings of self-worth must then be restored before any positive therapeutic effect can take place.

We do not intend to suggest that there is no place and no value in psychiatry or psychotherapy as generally practiced. Psychiatrists are specialists who are trained to treat seriously ill people and may well be wasting their talents treating those who are less disturbed. Even when referral is indicated, there are often serious impediments to many patients' receiving psychiatric treatment. Some are financial, some are logistical,[12] and some have to do with the patient's reluctance to pursue treatment. Regardless of these factors, we suggest that there are some very important psychotherapeutic interventions that are available to the primary care physician. Furthermore, we maintain that the interventions that can be made by the primary care physician are different in several respects from those generally employed by psychiatrists. Let us look at some of these differences.

Treatment of Symptoms without Psychiatric Labeling

The first major difference is that the primary care physician can treat the emotional reaction of the patient to whatever environmental stress is being experienced without labeling the patient as a mental patient. The patient receives the help that is asked for (relief of symptoms) and does not have to deal with the idea of seeing a "shrink." Actually, our experience has been that after working with the primary care physician on the emotional overlay attached to various physical problems, patients will often request a referral to a mental health practitioner in order to further their work of self-exploration. One of the more beneficial aspects of the therapeutic relationship with the primary care physician may be to prepare the patient for needed in-depth psychological treatment.[13] By making the patient aware of the benefits in the form of symptom relief and more effective functioning that result from increased levels of personal awareness, the patient may overcome a reluctance to engage in psychiatric treatment. However, for many patients the timely intervention of the physician helps to restore normal functioning or even improve functioning to such an extent as to preclude the need for further treatment.

Small Doses of Therapy at a Time

The second major difference between psychotherapy as practiced by the primary care physician and the psychiatrist is that the patient receives small doses of psychotherapy as a part of the regular medical treatment. Every part of the interaction of the patient with the physician is potentially therapeutic. We have gone to great lengths to point out the amount of social power attributed to physicians. The personal exchanges, both verbal and nonverbal, that occur during the normal office visit can have a tremendous impact on the patient. Since each of us has an assumptive map, a mental representation of ourselves and our world based on personal history as we have recorded it, our self-perception can be influenced by how we see ourselves being treated by significant others with whom we come in contact.[14-16] If our assumptive map tells us that we are not at all important but then, over time, we are repeatedly treated well by an important person, after some initial discounting and disbelief we may change our map. As the weight of evidence countering our preconceived notions of ourselves increases, we are able to make a change in our self-image. It may actually take the form of a paradigm shift, as explained in Chapter 1. Small, repeated doses of psychotherapeutic messages can sometimes be more effective, in terms of being heard, believed, and integrated, than a large dose at any one time, which may be more difficult to assimilate. People learn by repetition over a period of time, and only when they are ready and open.

The Patient Does Not Feel Rejected

The third major factor to be considered in providing psychological treatment personally rather than making a referral, even when appropriate, is that often the patient may interpret the referral as rejection. When a patient's self-esteem is at a low point and the physician responds by pushing the patient away, sending the patient to see someone else, this can confirm the patient's view that "no one can or wants to help." If the patient feels comfortable with and trusts the physician, there is a natural reluctance to start over with someone new. The patient may well feel that there is not much use in even trying. Being referred may well play into the patient's self-deprecating pathology. In contrast, the physician's commitment to helping the patient is interpreted as an indication that the situation may be far less serious than the patient had assumed and that the patient is much more worthy of help. Naturally, there will be times when a referral must be made because the physician feels overwhelmed. This will be discussed in a subsequent section.

The Body and the Mind Are Not Separated

Especially in the case of psychosomatic illness, rather than exploring all the organic elements before trying to convince the patient that psychological treatment is indicated, which can make the patient feel inadequate and raise resistance, we treat physical and psychological components of the problem concurrently, which may over time convince the patient of the connection. This moves the patient in a positive direction toward combating the underlying problem. Writing in the *New England Journal of Medicine* about functional gastrointestinal disorders, J. E. Leonard-Jones points out that it is essential to make the psychosocial history part of the initial inquiry "because a sudden interest in possible psychological factors after investigations have given normal results can arouse hostility in the patient."[17] Patients with psychosomatic problems who are referred to psychiatrists after a full exploration of their somatic complaints are notorious for seeking further medical opinions and being refractory to psychiatric treatment.[18,19] The focus on purely organic problems is not necessarily benign. Harrington has pointed out that physicians often unwittingly precipitate or perpetuate emotional illness in patients: "Every psychiatrist sees patients who have been in the hands of three or four different specialists, all of whom are said to have told the patient something different. Such patients are hard to treat because they have lost faith."[20]

THE PHYSICIAN-PATIENT RELATIONSHIP

There are several distinct differences in the way a patient relates to a primary care physician and to a psychiatrist. The relationship with the primary care physician has continuity over time and is predicated on receiving whatever care is necessary to keep the patient healthy and functioning at optimum levels. Patients' emotional responses are logical concomitants of their physical condition and can be treated as such. In contrast, a relationship with a psychiatrist is specifically focused on eradicating some mental aberration or personality defect that is interfering with the patient's ability to function. This interference must be serious enough to overcome the patient's resistance to psychiatric treatment.

The Effects of the Psychiatric Evaluation Process

The initial psychiatric interview is structured to establish rapport with the patient while determining the etiology and extent of the patient's psychopathology. The psychiatrist will draw inferences from the behavior of the patient toward the interviewer. Many people, not only psychiatric patients, feel very uncomfortable when they know that they are being analyzed. As a result they may become defensive. Patients who are sharing information about various aspects of their functioning with the primary care physician may feel much more sanguine about disclosing personal information. This may be especially true when the information is elicited in a series of visits.

Knowledge of the Family

The primary care physician often has had contact with various members of the patient's family. If the physician already knows the circumstances of a patient's family constellation and has had personal contact with the cast of characters involved, it becomes easier to empathize with the patient's experience. A statement such as, "Yes, I know Mary can be difficult to deal with. What can you do to make her feel more secure?", can be a powerful intervention when it comes from someone who has had dealings with Mary. The patient already trusts the physician while the psychiatrist is an unknown who is suspect simply because of being cast in the role of psychiatrist, that is, an evaluator and analyst.

The Gift of Caring

Perhaps the most crucial difference in the character of the primary care physician-patient relationship as opposed to the psychiatrist-patient relationship is that in the former whatever psychological support is received is seen as a bonus. Although it may not always be intuitively obvious, there is a difference between psychological support that is received and that which is given. We are not always open to the positive messages that are directed at us. It is necessary to be open to hearing supportive statements. If self-esteem is exceedingly low, being told by another that we are perfectly capable, and will be OK is interpreted as false reassurance and a further confirmation that no one understands just how dreadful we feel and how awful everything is.

A patient seeks psychiatric treatment in order to feel better. The patient expects the psychiatrist to be helpful and provide support. Actually, the psychiatrist may be far more interested in making a diagnosis and prescribing pharmacological treatment. A physician is expected to provide medical diagnosis and treatment. Williard Gaylin, in his insightful book, *Caring*,[21] discusses the importance of finding outlets to express the caring impulse, which is biologically programmed into the human species, and makes the following point that helps clarify the impact of the physician's interest in the psychological adjustment of the patient.

> We are generally touched by behavior that does more for us than we might have expected, [and] we are hurt by behavior that does less for us than we feel we have a right to expect. It is my feeling that in most senses of the usage, being touched and feeling hurt are polar phenomena. I am touched by your solicitude and hurt by your lack of solicitude; touched by the fact that despite a limited acquaintance, you remembered my birthday; hurt by the fact that even though you are my spouse, you had forgotten. If being touched is preeminently visualized in terms of the delighted and somewhat unexpected caring attitude of an individual, feeling hurt is the absence of such an attitude where we feel entitled to it and where we have every reason to expect it. In that sense we can see where we are more likely to be hurt by those who are close to us and touched by casual friends. In both cases there is an unexpected and unwarranted quality. Those who know us slightly honor us with their

affection or attention, as those who know us well abuse us by failing to show that they care. To feel hurt occurs with a failure in caring. This, then, represents our vulnerability through attachments, or need to feel cared for.[21]

If the psychiatrist fails to give the expected support or appears to be cold and distant, the patient feels hurt. On the other hand, the physician's interest in the psychological aspect of the patient's condition is received as a gift of caring. The patient is generally touched and this touch is healing. The bonus for the practicing physician is that the patient responds positively to the physician, thereby increasing compliance and satisfaction for both parties.

THE PHYSICIAN'S VIEW OF THE PATIENT

The primary care physician has the special opportunity and responsibility to relate to the patient not just from either a physiological or psychological perspective. Our approach to the patient is based on the assumption that the basic biological unit reacting to the demands from the environment encompasses the body, mind, and spirit in dynamic interaction. This is hardly a revolutionary idea. Twenty-five years ago, John Nemiah, a noted professor of psychiatry at Harvard Medical School, wrote as follows:

> The practitioner who limits himself, whether it be to the confines of physiology or psychology, does so to the detriment of his patient. The art and practice of medicine requires on the part of the doctor an awareness that human life is a process lived in a constantly changing world which requires, for survival, a constantly adaptive response. . . . Rational treatment is based on helping the patient return to health by combatting the forces upsetting the balance—whether physiological or psychological.[22]

The role of the primary care practitioner is to understand that the mind and body together constitute the complete unit of the individual who is integrally influenced by stimuli from external and internal environments. By being able to engage the person psychologically while laying on hands in the process of examining the body, the physician is in a unique position to help the patient correct whatever disturbance in homeostasis has precipitated the visit to the doctor.

The psychiatrist, on the other hand, is more narrowly focused on the psychodynamics of the personality. If we go back to the model proposed in Chapter 2, where *person plus stress yields reaction*, the psychiatrist is dealing primarily with the *person* variable. Also, by emphasizing the mind instead of the body, the reverse split achieves no more productive result than looking for pathology only in tissues and organs. The tendency to specialize fragments the ability to care for the person. It may well be that the fragmentation in the fabric of our society or the structure of the patient's family or work situation is precipitating the illness in the first place. The changing model of health care (see Chapter 1) requires that the body, mind, and spirit be integrated, since a demoralized patient can maintain neither physical nor mental health.

In *Megatrends*,[23] a book about emerging transitions in American society in the '80s, John Naisbitt points to the need to shift the focus from specialists who quickly become obsolete to generalists who can adapt. Not only do we have to help our patients adapt to the everchanging environment, but as Naisbitt also points out, there is a deeply felt need for personal, high-touch care, especially in the fields such as medicine where technology is advancing at a particularly rapid pace.

So the major difference in the approach of the primary care physician, in contrast to that of the psychiatrist, is to help the patient make a more comfortable adaptation to the existing environment without getting into the specific technicalities of the patient's personality structure, specific defense mechanisms, or even family dynamics, since these are difficult to change (except in a crisis). Instead, the physician focuses on the reaction that the person is experiencing to perceived stress from the environment. This reaction may be anxiety, depression, and/or any number of physical complaints. By providing support and focusing the patient on constructive action, the physician helps to enhance the patient's self-esteem and enables the patient to function at a more productive level.

THE PHYSICIAN'S VIEW OF THE PROBLEM

Perhaps the most important factor to keep in mind when doing psychotherapy in the fifteen minute framework is that the problem belongs to the patient. The physician cannot afford to get intimately involved in the details of the problem, understand the exact etiology, or even the specific effect of the problem on all the people involved. The physician is not responsible for solving the problem. However, the physician is responsible for making the patient identify a specific problem that may be underlying the experienced stress, making the patient aware that this problem is contributing to the feelings of illness that the patient is experiencing, and encouraging the patient to explore potential solutions for this problem.

In *Megatrends*,[23] there is a report that the direction to self-help as opposed to institutional help is one of the strongest emerging trends in our society. The type of behavior that is manifested when people take responsibility for resolving their own problems is to be encouraged. Naisbitt claims that the most reliable way to anticipate, and therefore be prepared to deal effectively with the future, is to understand what is happening in the present. Physicians must understand the forces that are moving people in the direction of self-help and self-responsibility. When we go with the flow, we are much more likely to be successful than when we try to resist a trend. The trend toward self-responsibility is healthy and can be encouraged by physicians by providing support and positive expectations regarding patients' management of problems.

When the physician communicates to the patient that there is the expectation that the patient, having identified the problem, is expected to find some constructive resolution, a positive message is conveyed. The physician agrees to be part of the process, to make suggestions for strategies that can be employed, but it is clear to both parties that the patient has the responsibility to deal with the problem—which by definition is expected to yield to resolution.

Focus on the Here and Now

Our approach, which focuses almost exclusively on the present, is very different from the usual psychiatric focus on the past. Patients are much less concerned about understanding the origins of their complaints than about getting relief in the present and having something positive to anticipate. There have been several influential advocates for physicians engaging patients in psychotherapeutic relationships.[18,20,24] Most notable is Michael Balint, who taught physicians to look at themselves and their interactions with patients to determine the therapeutic or countertherapeutic effects based on a psychoanalytic orientation. His seminal volume, *The Doctor, His Patient and the Illness*,[18] has helped many physicians understand some of the dynamics of the therapeutic encounter that interfere or promote the patient's response to treatment. In this text and the subsequent volume by Balint and Norell, *Six Minutes for the Patient*,[25] which promotes making one really insightful comment during each medical interview, Balint underscores the importance of understanding the psychodynamics of both the patient's and the physician's personality structures from an analytical orientation. Balint[18] suggests that in order for physicians to deal effectively with patients' psychological problems, a change in their personality may be required. We are really less ambitious! We suggest that physicians only need to engage in specific behaviors, since changing behavior (to include cognitive processes) is much more feasible than changing personality structures.

In *The Twenty Minute Hour*, Castelnuovo-Tedesco[24] also encourages physicians to address patients' emotional difficulties as an integral part of the medical interview in order to enhance the value of treatment. This author suggests that primary care physicians need to understand psychotherapeutic treatment and do brief therapy with selected patients. Our approach is to integrate the emotional aspects routinely with *all* patients. Castelnuovo-Tedesco suggests that brief therapy needs to be planned in order to deal systematically with the interpersonal aspects of the patient's life. This implies a comprehensive and accurate analysis of the dynamics involved. Unfortunately, studies have not borne out the efficacy of this treatment approach by general practitioners.[26] Many physicians may mistakenly cite the failure of this type of therapy in general medical practice as a justification for not engaging their patients psychotherapeutically. Our approach does not require *detailed* knowledge of a wide range of emotional disorders. It does not require an understanding of the etiology of the patient's discomfort. It does require the ability to recognize the symptoms and provide psychological support for the patient's healthy functioning mechanisms.

Castelnuovo-Tedesco[24] sees classical psychoanalytical treatment as ultimately the most effective psychotherapeutic modality. Our approach integrates several newer techniques coming from crisis intervention, stress management, and cognitive, behavioral, and existential literature. Abreaction and insight have unfortunately not been shown to be more effective in combating psychological distress than have the direct approaches we are promoting.[27]

The last point made by Castelnuovo-Tedesco[24] is that when physicians do twenty minute therapy, patients do not develop transference because of the limited time involved. We contend, quite to the contrary, that patients bring to the physician a highly developed and integrated transference relationship consisting of their expectations from benevolent authority figures. This power, which is ceded by the patient, can be used to enhance the therapeutic relationship.

Focus on the Patient's Strength

The essence of supportive therapy is to restore patients' faith in their own capacity to take charge of their lives in a productive and satisfying way. Every difficult situation is a variation on some previous situation. If patients had not survived these earlier traumas, they would not be presenting themselves at this time. The physician's job is to remind the patient about having overcome past obstacles. This enhances the sense of coherence.[28] Then together they can factor out those techniques previously found successful. If patterns have consistently been destructive, then patients must be encouraged to make some small change in the way that they would normally react.

Each of us has a rather limited behavioral repertoire. In any situation, there is some way that we naturally respond because that is what we have learned to do under those specific circumstances. When we do not get the expected or desired result, we often redouble our efforts and keep doing whatever we are doing, longer and harder. We have what psychologists call a limited response set. The physician can suggest that the patient make a small change in the current behavioral pattern, with the expectation that there will then be a change in the resulting outcome. This change can be expected to be positive. Again, where the psychiatrist might focus on exploring why and how these behavioral patterns emerged, we would focus on what is in it for the patient to maintain the pattern in the here and now. If this turned out to be nothing or pain, then we would encourage the patient to change the behavioral repertoire. We would encourage the patient to act in some new and different way, develop a broader response set, and monitor the result.

Involving the Patient's Family

Primary care physicians' special relationships with patients and the patients' families enable them to invite other family members to work with the patient in addressing whatever problem is most disturbing. Where the analyst is invested in helping the patient understand reactions to significant others, we would focus on making communications more open and direct, helping patients express feelings and ask for what they want. We would provide the knowledge that we do not always get what we want but that by identifying our desires and stating them, the probability of gratification is enhanced. We would encourage patients to explore options with their families and teach strategies for conflict resolution and problem solving. We would make everyone aware that a problem that is experienced by one member of a family has impact on all other family members. We would charge them to discuss the matter and then report back to us.

THE THERAPEUTIC APPROACH

The most important aspect of the therapeutic relationship is the physician's show of concern. This is concern for the patient as a person and for the patient as a member of a family. The physician can show concern through the use of a variety of techniques.

Giving Empathy

Carl Rogers[29] suggests that in order for constructive personality change to take place, the following conditions need to be met and sustained over time.

1. Two persons need to be in a psychological relationship with one person specifically dedicated to helping the other. The physician, in this case, should experience "unconditional positive regard" for the patient.
2. The person in the therapeutic role experiences an empathetic understanding of the patient's internal frame of reference and is able to communicate this understanding along with the positive regard to the patient "at least to a minimum degree."

We propose that the physician needs to make a personal commitment to help patients cope with the emotional aspects of their lives. This commitment may entail an adjustment in the map of what it means to be a good physician. The personal choice to engage the patient establishes the psychological relationship that Carl Rogers specifies to

Approaches to Therapy

be the prerequisite for therapeutic change. It also demonstrates the positive regard that the physician has for the patient. This commitment becomes actualized by the physician's inquiring how the patient feels about what is going on in his or her life. It establishes the context of the visit and redefines the limits of the physician's interest. Having determined how the patient feels and what the patient is most concerned about, the physician communicates the understanding of the patient's affective state through making an empathetic response. Rogers' two conditions have thus been met. If this process is repeated during every patient visit, the cumulative effect can be positive change in the patient's self-image and ability to cope constructively.

Exploring Options

The second basic technique that physicians can incorporate into a brief office visit is to ask patients about their options. In many cases, people who are caught in a painful emotional situation are not aware that there are always options. Naturally, each potential choice has consequences, but awareness of the power to choose (even if it only affects our attitude) makes us feel less impotent and overwhelmed.

In the early 1970s, Stanley Milgram[30] performed an experiment to determine people's response to authority. An experimenter demanded that subjects behave in a manner to put another person at great risk. The experiment was disguised as a learning task and the subjects were ordered to apply shock to a stooge who pretended to be adversely affected by this treatment. Subjects routinely followed orders, though uncomfortable, especially after passing into a range of shock marked "danger". A movie was made in which the interactions between subject, experimenter, and stooge could be observed. Although most subjects performed as directed when they were simply told "You must continue with the experiment," in those cases where the experimenter added, "You have no choice," subjects invariably stopped—said something to the effect that of course they had a choice. They could walk out. And then they walked out. It seemed that just having the word choice mentioned tuned them in to the fact that there were options.

Most people looking back on what seem to be serious mistakes made during turning points in their lives will say that it never occurred to them that there was any other option. It is extremely helpful to remind patients that at any time they always have choices, and one of them may be not to decide at that particular time, to choose not to choose, at least for now. Having the physician suggest that there are options, that the patient can go home and list them and come back to discuss things further, is a powerful therapeutic technique.

Encouraging New Behavior

Another powerful tool available to the physician is to encourage patients to change certain behavioral patterns and engage in potentially more productive interactions with others. Although specific advice is generally to be discouraged (the physician should not take responsibility for solving the problem or give the patient the opportunity to sabotage), the options of taking time out, deciding not to decide, expressing feelings and asking for what is wanted, keeping a diary to document periods of heightened stress, or noting eating or sleeping patterns, are all strategies that promote new behavior. Once patients become aware of their power to change their behavior and receive subsequent reinforcement from the environment, these positive changes can be sustained. The patient's verbal commitment to the physician that certain new ways of acting will be adopted in specific situations can give the patient a powerful push in new and constructive directions.

Providing Explanations

The physician's acceptance of the patient's difficulties in a particular situation can be a great source of relief. The physician makes what have been called ubiquity statements. These consist of pointing out that generally people who are undergoing situations common to what the patient is experiencing will react by feeling overwhelmed and acting in potentially destructive ways, saying that under these circumstances a person would feel very angry or that it is common to want to walk out and let the other people cope with the mess. By explaining to a patient that under certain circumstances (e.g., unemployment, bereavement, birth of a child, separation, divorce, illness, promotion, moving, graduating, child launching, etc.) people are naturally more vulnerable and easily go on *tilt*, patients may feel more comfortable with their reactions. Once they feel secure that they are reacting normally, it may be much easier for them to control their behavior. Sometimes it may be necessary to explain to patients that children, spouses, or employers also have certain needs and that it may well be necessary for the patient to come to terms with unwanted changes in the interpersonal environment. The patient is reassured that it is not necessary to like the situation but that it is necessary to learn to deal with it. Patients also need to be told that they can feel in certain ways without having to do anything about it.

Giving Anticipatory Guidance

One of the most promising therapeutic opportunities available to the primary care physician concerns the ability to give anticipatory guidance. Anticipating problems allows people to devise strategies for coping with the problems, before they arise. It also gives them time to readjust attitudes, if necessary. When situations do not develop suddenly and present as a shock, coping behavior can be more appropriate and more mature. Instead of saying, "Isn't this awful," the patient will realize, "Goodness, I feel just like the doctor said I might. Isn't that interesting!"

Since the physician sees the patient over time, anticipatory guidance regarding expected life-cycle crises or other situations can be incorporated into routine visits for school physicals: "Have you thought about how you're going to feel when Mary is in school all day?" "How do you suppose you're going to feel once Sam Jr. goes off to college?" During prenatal visits the physician can say: "You know, having a baby is going to change many aspects of your life. You and Henry need to carefully plan in order to assure private time for the two of you." During general physicals the physician may comment: "This promotion is going to involve a lot of travel, as I hear it. Have you discussed with Debbie how this will affect your relationship?" "Now that you are going back to school, I would encourage you to plan to spend quality time with each of the children regularly. You do not need to feel guilty about spending less time, if you make sure that they each get some direct positive attention daily." "Jane, now that you are going to be alone, you may find it very difficult at first. You may have trouble sleeping and not have much appetite. I expect that there will be times that you will be overcome by angry feelings toward Charles. That is all normal, although that doesn't make it feel any better."

Making Contact at an Early Phase of the Problem

Probably the most significant difference between the approach of the primary care physician and the psychiatrist is that the physician sees the patient much earlier in the process of a developing problem, usually for medical symptoms. It has been pointed out[31] that often the attempts that we make to solve problems become more of a problem than the original difficulty. Drinking to forget our troubles or relieve anxiety, running away, making threats that are taken seriously, holding feelings in, setting unenforceable limits, and engaging in power struggles are only a few examples. By seeing the patient when the situation is still fluid, the intervention by the physician can sometimes prevent dire consequences (primary prevention) or reduce the severity of consequences (secondary prevention) or at least prevent further complications (tertiary prevention.)

THE EFFECTS OF BRIEF SESSIONS

The most obvious difference between the type of therapy we are promoting and the usual fifty minute therapeutic hour is the time limitation that we have imposed. We feel strongly that the physician should try to limit encounters with the patient to a quarter of an hour. By only spending a few minutes during the regular medical interview to deal with the psychological aspect of the patient's situation, only one or two points can be made. Our experience has been that this has a very powerful effect. Since a person under stress has a limited capacity to concentrate and process new information, dealing with only one or two issues has a beneficial effect in not putting the patient on overload.

Setting Priorities

When the patient becomes familiar with the physician's style and expects the inquiry, another benefit is achieved. The patient learns to arrange issues in order of priority. This process of organization is helpful and therapeutic for the patient. It forces the patient to evaluate problems in terms of severity and urgency. The patient chooses the particular issue to be brought up at each session. In looking forward to reporting about the experience since the previous visit (while considering the limits of time), the patient is forced to summarize and focus on the high points. It is always interesting to inquire about successes as well as failures and disappointments.

Homework Is Essential

Homework is an essential part of the therapeutic fifteen minute hour, since the brief time available must be used most efficiently. By giving the patient specific assignments, self-help and new behavior is encouraged, enhancing the patient's self-esteem and sense of competence. For example, the patient can be asked to make lists of options, resources, advantages, disadvantages, arguments, things that are bothersome, things that are desired, and previous accomplishments. The patient can also be asked to keep diaries documenting periods of being upset, diets, sleep patterns, successful coping, the best thing that happened each day, the worst thing that happened each day, and problems and potential solutions. The patient can be asked to do one new thing each day.

The effectiveness of the homework assignment is enhanced by having the patient make a contract to carry out the assigned task. By communicating the joint expectation that the patient will return with the assignment successfully completed, the sense of connectedness to the physician is completed. The physician's interest and concern is clearly demonstrated, as is the physician's faith in the patient's resolve to tackle the assignment. It is important that assignments be simple and feasible. In this way the physician is underscoring the two essential needs of the patient—the need to have a sense of personal competence and the need to be connected to another human being.

The brief session is also beneficial because it minimizes the patient's dependence on the physician and maximizes the patient's own resources, while providing a source of support. Patients feel that they have a partner in their search for problem resolution and that this partner is someone who cares enough to follow and encourage their progress.

REFERRAL

Once patients become aware of some of their inter- or intrapersonal difficulties in certain situations, they may well feel that they would like to explore their psychological functioning to a greater depth. Perhaps the behavior of one family member makes the family aware that the particular dynamics that have become established are not constructive and that family therapy (restructuring) is indicated. Perhaps the physician feels that a particular patient would benefit from seeing a practitioner for lengthier sessions to work through some deep-seated conflicts. Perhaps an unresolved grief reaction truly needs an in-depth exploration of the elements of a complex relationship. In all of these cases, the physician has the option of referring the patient after first assuring the patient that the physician will continue to serve as the primary care provider. The physician will continue to be concerned with what is happening to the patient. In this case, what is happening is treatment by a psychiatrist.

Other options available to the physician include referral to a variety of practitioners in the community. These might include public agencies or self-help groups like AA or Al Anon, UNITE, Amend, HOPE, SHARE, Compassionate Friends, CancerCare, Alzheimer's support groups, and social groups like Parents Without Partners. There are also a wide variety of mental health professionals—from psychiatrists, psychologists, social workers, nurse practitioners, and pastoral counselors to biofeedback technicians—to whom the physician can refer.

In any case, the physician's commitment to the patient is to provide that care that can be given within the physician's expertise. The ability to provide psychological support as we have outlined it is well within most physicians' expertise and can be expected to yield effective results. By refraining from analyzing or explaining the origin of behavior and helping the patient focus on managing reactions to situations, the physician's approach is quite different from that of a traditional psychiatrist. However, it is highly effective.

SUMMARY

There are differences between the therapeutic approaches of the primary care physician and the psychiatrist in the areas of patient expectations and reactions, the nature of the therapeutic relationship, and the physician's investment in the patient's problem. Defining themselves as mental patients carries costs that patients do not incur when treated by their physician. Symptoms can be treated without psychiatric labels. Small doses of therapy at a time may prove quite effective. The patient does not feel rejected, and the body and mind are not separated.

The relationship with the primary care physician has continuity, rapport is established nonjudgmentally, and knowledge of the family enhances the physician's effectiveness. The physician's support and interest is seen as a bonus. The primary care physician, in contrast to the psychiatrist, makes the patient more comfortable in adapting to the existing environment, without getting into the technicalities of the patient's personality structure, specific defense mechanisms, or even family dynamics, since these are difficult to change.

The physician contracts to help the patient identify specific problems and expects that the patient will find some constructive resolution. This conveys a positive message. Attention is focused almost exclusively in the here and now, on the patient's strength, and involves the family. The therapeutic approach consists of using empathy, exploring options, encouraging new behavior, providing explanations, and giving anticipatory guidance. Probably the most significant difference between the approach of the primary care physician and the psychiatrist is that the physician sees the patient much earlier in the process of a developing problem, usually for medical symptoms. The time limit of the sessions helps the patient to set priorities, necessitates homework, and minimizes the patient's dependence on the physician. Referral remains an option and can be facilitated by the preparatory process.

REFERENCES

1. McHugh, P. R. and Slavney, P. R. *The Perspectives of Psychiatry*. Baltimore: Johns Hopkins University Press, 1983.
2. American Psychiatric Association: *Diagnostic and Statistical Manual of Mental Disorders*, 3rd ed. Washington, D.C.: American Psychiatric Association, 1980.
3. Carpenter, P. J., Morrow, G. R., Del Gaudio, A. C., and Ritzler, B. A. Who keeps the first outpatient appointment? *American Journal of Psychiatry*, 1981, *138*, 102–105.
4. Rosenberg, C. and Rayes, A. *Keeping Patients in Psychiatric Treatment*. Cambridge, MA: Ballinger, 1976.
5. Baekland, I. and Lundwall, L. Dropping out of treatment. A critical review. *Psychological Bulletin*, 1975, *82*, 738–783.
6. Koss, M. P. Length of psychotherapy for clients seen in private practice. *Journal of Consulting Clinical Psychology*, 1979, *47*, 210–212.
7. Rockwell, K. W. J. and Pinkerton, R. S. Single-session psychotherapy. *American Journal of Psychotherapy*, 1982, *36*, 32–40.

8. Bowden, C. L., Schoenfeld, L. S., and Adams, R. L. A correlation between dropout status and improvement in a psychiatric clinic. *Hospital & Community Psychiatry*, 1980, *31*, 192–195.

9. Szasz, T. S. The myth of mental illness. *American Psychologist*, 1960, *15*, 113–118.

10. Halleck, S. L. *The Politics of Therapy*. New York: Science House, 1971.

11. Gorenstein, E. E. Debating mental illness: Implications for science, medicine, and social policy. *American Psychologist*, 1984, *39*, 40–49.

12. Lee, S. H. Gianturco, D. T., and Eisdorfer, C. Community mental health center accessibility. *Archives of General Psychiatry*, 1974, *31*, 335–339.

13. Larson, D. L., Nguyen, T. D., Green, R. S., and Attkisson, C. C. Enhancing the utilization of outpatient mental health services. *Community Mental Health Journal*, 1983, 305–320.

14. Angyal, A. *Neurosis and Treatment: A Holistic Theory*. New York: Wiley, 1965.

15. Bandler, R. and Grinder, J. *The Structure of Magic I: A Book about Language and Therapy*. Palo Alto, CA: Science and Behavior Books, 1975.

16. Bateson, G. *Steps to an Ecology of Mind*. New York: Ballantine Books, 1972.

17. Lennard-Jones, J. E., Functional gastrointestinal disorders. *New England Journal of Medicine*, 1983, *308*, 431–435.

18. Balint, M. *The Doctor, His Patient and the Illness*: New York: International Universities Press, 1957.

19. Adler, G. The physician and the hypochondriacal patient. *New England Journal of Medicine*, 1981, *304*, 1394–1396.

20. Harrington, J. A. Some principles of psychotherapy in general practice. *Lancet*, 1957, *1*, 799–780.

21. Gaylin. W. *Caring*. New York: Knopf, 1976, p. 152.

22. Nemiah, J. C. *Foundations of Psychopathology*. New York: Oxford University Press, 1961, p. 289.

23. Naisbitt, J. *Megatrends: Ten New Directions Transforming Our Lives*. New York: Warner Books, 1982.

24. Castelnuovo-Tedesco, P. *The Twenty Minute Hour*. Boston: Little, Brown, 1965.

25. Balint, E. and Norell, J. S., eds. *Six Minutes for the Patient: Interactions in General Practice Consultation*. London: Tavistock, 1973.

26. Brodaty, H. and Andrews, G. Brief psychotherapy in family practice: A controlled prospective intervention trial. *British Journal of Psychiatry*, 1983, *143*, 11–19.

27. Epstein, N. B. and Vlok, L. A. Research on the results of psychotherapy: A summary of evidence. *American Journal of Psychiatry*, 1981, *138*, 1027–1035.

28. Antonovsky, A. *Health, Stress, and Coping*. San Francisco: Jossey-Bass, 1979.

29. Rogers, C. R. The necessary and sufficient conditions of therapeutic personality change. *Journal of Consulting Psychology*, 1957, *21*, 95–103.

30. Milgrim, S. Behavioral study of obedience. *Journal of Abnormal and Social Psychology*, 1963, *67*, 371–378.

31. Watzlawick, P., Weakland, J., and Fisch, R. *Change: Principles of Problem Formation and Problem Resolution*. New York: Norton, 1974.

6
The Structure of Therapy

Are we really suggesting that the patient's psychological needs should be addressed during *every* patient visit? Yes, we are! Just as physicians are familiar with the rather extensive body of literature dealing with the advantages of periodic health screening from an organic perspective, we are convinced that assessing a person's emotional state on the occasion of each visit can provide many of the same benefits. Not only that, but our experience is that these needs can be addressed efficiently and effectively.

DEFINING THE STRUCTURE OF THERAPY

In previous chapters we have pointed out the importance and unique opportunity inherent in the doctor-patient relationship for dealing with the emotional needs of the patient. The physician dealing with the psychological aspect of a patient's problem must focus on organizing the psychotherapeutic intervention into the regular fifteen minute visit. The goal is to help the patients reorganize some small aspect of their self-concept or behavior in a more comfortable, productive, or, at minimum, less destructive manner.

Therapy grows out of the already established physician-patient relationship. Patients have certain preconceived notions of how the physician sees them, as well as how they see the physician. Therefore, it follows that the physician is in an excellent position to apply psychotherapeutic principles. The treatment is aimed at affecting patients' images of themselves, their problems, and their options, adjusting some aspect of their assumptive world view. Good interviewing techniques, a caring manner, and genuine interest demonstrated by paying serious attention and concentrating on the patient's problems pave the way toward establishing a psychologically therapeutic milieu. In the process, patients feel supported, less stressed, and are able to raise their level of self-esteem as well as reengage their healthier coping styles.[1] The physician not only gains a healthier and more reasonable patient, but by applying this technique with its small investment of time during each patient visit, the physician may save a tremendous amount of time in some future encounter. If a patient's unaddressed psychological needs are allowed to compound over time, they can become overwhelming. The patient's expressed needs at that time may overextend the physician's resources to deal with a monumental problem.

DETERMINING THE CONTEXT OF THE VISIT

Optimally, every physical complaint or office visit should be seen in the context of the patient's and his or her family's total life situation. To make this determination, the physician must include in the current history an exploration of what is going on in the patient's life in addition to descriptions of presenting symptoms that may well represent a response to a situational stress.

Recently, many primary care physicians have been organizing their charts around the problem-oriented medical record.[2] Problems are listed and notes are organized in *soap* fashion. We are all familiar with the system that arranges progress notes into subjective, objective, assessment, and plan elements. To understand the patients' problems in the context of their total life situation, primary care physicians need a larger concept of *soap*.[3] The total package of patient assessment also requires determination of the background situation, the patient's affect, what is troubling the patient, and a determination of how the patient is handling the stress. The acronym BATHE connotes memory jogs for handling the context of the visit.

B stands for background. A simple question, "What is going on in your life?", will elicit the context of the patient's visit.

A stands for affect (the feeling state). "How do you feel about what is going on?" or "What's your mood?" allows the patient to report the current feeling state.

T stands for trouble. "What about the situation troubles you the most?" helps both the physician and the patient focus.

H stands for handling. "How are you handling that?" gives an assessment of functioning.

The Structure of Therapy

Following this information gathering, an understanding response is required to provide closure.

E stands for empathy. "That must be very difficult for you" legitimizes the patient's feelings.

By BATHEing the patient early in the visit, an effective and efficient psychotherapeutic intervention is structured into every patient encounter. The context of the visit has been incorporated into the session and there is closure. The physician then proceeds with the appropriate physical examination. If necessary, additional support and/or provision for follow-up is structured into the latter part of the visit.

> A 34-year-old woman, who had been a patient at the family practice center for about a year, presented in the office complaining about a vaginal discharge. She appeared to be quite agitated. The physician inquired about what was going on in her life. The patient started to cry.
> "I just found out that my husband has been having an affair with my oldest sister for the past year and a half."
> "How do you feel about that?" (The physician felt a little foolish. It seemed like this was an inane question to ask under the circumstances—but he really didn't know what else to ask.)
> "I feel angry. I have mood swings. I go up and down. I also feel depressed."
> The physician then asked what about the situation troubled the patient the most. She replied, "I have two children. They are two and five, and I really don't want to be a single parent."
> (The physician was surprised. He would have expected her to be most troubled because of the familial involvement or the time frame.)
> "How are you handling it?", was his final question.
> The patient felt that she was handling things very badly. She was angry and did a lot of shouting at her husband. She also added that she was afraid that the children were starting to be affected and that she did not want that.
> The physician, was taken aback by this history. Still, he managed to respond, "That sounds like a horrendous situation."
> "Yes, it is," said the patient and visibly relaxed.
> "Why don't we examine you now, and find out what we can do about your vaginal discomfort," said the physician, "and then we'll talk some more."

Supporting the Patient

In Chapter 2 we defined social support as a psychological mechanism that provides positive information to the individual about his or her interaction with other people. Social support can be seen as encompassing one or more of the following: (1) an expression of positive affect, (2) an endorsement of the person's behavior, perception, or expressed views, (3) giving symbolic or material aid, and (4) giving the opportunity to express feelings in an accepting atmosphere.

Gerald Caplan[4] suggests that social support is of a continuing nature as the outgrowth of an enduring relationship. The particular elements of support stressed by Caplan include (1) helping the individual to mobilize his or her own resources, (2) helping in sharing tasks, (3) helping in providing information or guidance to facilitate handling of the situation, and (4) providing material supplies or skills to affect the situation.

It is clear that by BATHEing the patient with every visit, many of the above criteria are satisfied. Interest and positive affect have been expressed. Feelings have been accepted. Information is gathered that helps both patient and physician understand the patient's reaction, and the diagnosis becomes a large part of the "cure." Clearly defining the problem helps focus the patient and the physician on the resources necessary to reach a resolution.

Dealing with Multiple Problems

Often the physician encounters multiple problems in the course of interviewing a patient. Here, again, having a practical structure for dealing with them is helpful in keeping the physician focused and meeting the patient's needs. If an unexpected emotional response occurs during the interview, the physician finds out what is going on, explores the issue with three questions, and effects closure with an empathetic statement. In this way, a simple technique, sequentially applied, can effectively be used to handle complex situations. The following case, which was reported by one of our senior residents, is illustrative of the principles we are promoting.

> A new patient, a 38-year-old woman, presented with multiple concerns, including contraception, vaginal itching, dyspareunia, and

frequent headaches. On further questioning, she revealed that she was a working mother of three teenage children, widowed six years previously, and remarried one year ago. Family history was positive for hypertension and diabetes in grandparents and multiple sclerosis in her mother. The mother was currently 56 and had been in a nursing home for 12 years. At this point in the interview, the patient appeared tearful but attempted to suppress the tears. I asked her what was going on, and then used the rest of the *BATHE* technique. The patient started to cry saying that she had not cried for years about her mother. I asked her what her mom had been like. She stated she had always admired her mother's energy and unselfishness, which was why she felt so guilty about having her in the nursing home. I empathized and we went on. Subsequently, I found out that her mother's diagnosis had been made at the age of 38. I asked her what she thought might be causing her headaches. She said I shouldn't think she was crazy, but she had considered whether it might not be MS. I supported her by telling her that that was a natural concern under the circumstances and that I would do a thorough evaluation in that regard.

At this point, about 10 minutes into the interview, I pointed out that she had come with quite a few concerns and asked her which *one* she wanted most to deal with in this visit. She stated that she was most concerned about her vaginal itch. After some routine questions regarding the GU system, I asked how this condition was affecting her sexuality, to which she replied that she and her husband had not slept together in six months! She stated that she suspected him of having an affair. Six months ago also corresponded to the anniversary of her first husband's death. I asked a background question about the circumstances of her marriage and again finished the *BATHE* sequence. I then asked her to prepare for the physical examination and assured her I would check for venereal disease. She appeared relieved and revealed that she herself had had a "fling" just prior to the onset of the itching.

During the physical exam, I did enough of a review of systems to assure myself that her headaches were not of an immediately serious nature and I reassured her regarding her pelvic exam. I supported her by stating that she seemed to be handling things well under such stressful circumstances. I asked her to make an appointment for evaluation of her headaches and further discussion of her other concerns, including contraception. I asked her if she had any questions and she said, no, but she was very relieved after talking with me.

The entire session lasted 25 minutes.

In this case, the physician sequentially dealt with a variety of problems, both related to present circumstances and to unresolved grief from the past. By repeatedly using the BATHE structure, she dealt with these problems in a timely and sensitive manner.

THE USE OF MEDICATION

We have talked very little about the role of medication. It is up to the individual physician to determine how and when to prescribe pharmacological treatment to ease the patient's symptoms. In general, if the patient's acute distress is so severe as to seriously interfere with the patient's functioning, we would suggest treatment with short-acting anxiolitics, something to help the patient sleep and restore some measure of equilibrium. In treating depression, we would certainly encourage the combination of psychotropic medication along with psychotherapy. Studies have shown conclusively that the combination of treatment is consistently more effective than either modality by itself.[5]

However, for the chronic patient, treating the symptoms without seriously addressing the causes perpetuates the patient's sense of impotence. A prescription for Valium does nothing to fix a bad marriage where communications have broken down. However, if the patient is requesting medication, an ongoing negotiation may be required to titrate the medication over time.

USING DIFFERENT APPROACHES FOR CHRONIC AND ACUTE PROBLEMS

In an earlier chapter, we discussed models of helping and coping that are internally coherent models in people's heads—establishing whose fault a problem is and whose responsibility it is to fix it.[6] In terms of making therapeutic intervention, there are two models that are useful, practical, and effective: the compensatory model and the medical model. The compensatory model appears to be most useful with chronic problems, while the medical model lends itself best to acute situations, and/or very dependent patients.

The Compensatory Model Is for Chronic Problems

Using the compensatory model as a guide, the assumption is made that people are not responsible for creating their own problems in general, but are responsible for finding solutions. They need to find constructive ways of handling difficult or painful situations. In dealing with patients having chronic problems, this is a very useful approach. The removal of blame for creation of the problem is therapeutic. It raises the level of self-esteem. There is no blame placed for developing chronic conditions or in being in a position where chronic problems exist. However, the physician suggests that the patient is responsible for and capable of dealing with these problems realistically and finding solutions. The physician is there to help, to be a sounding board, and to head the cheering section. The positive expectation of the patient's ability to resolve the problem—the infusion of hope—is a powerful therapeutic tool.

Actually, the physician may think that the patient is responsible for creating the problem, as in the case of the 38-year-old woman who had had a fling; however, pointing this out is rarely therapeutic since it underscores the patient's sense of hopelessness and self-deprecation. As an example of this situation, consider the commonly encountered problem of recurrent headaches. If, after appropriate study, a determination is made that these headaches are in fact of the tension variety, having to do with the patient's reaction to her current life situation, then applying the inherently nonjudgmental *compensatory model* as a part of the therapeutic strategy and enlisting the patient's aid in resolving the conflicts that cause these symptoms can be much more clinically efficacious than just medicating the symptomatology. The patient is expected to learn to identify causes of stress. It is assumed that the patient has not been personally responsible for having created them. The patient will be expected to label the situation as a problem and to devise potential solutions. In addition, the patient will be expected to make those changes in behavior necessary to effect the most constructive outcome. Finally, the patient will also be expected to learn some stress management techniques and to practice them regularly.

The Medical Model Is for Acute Problems

With the medical model, the assumption is made that people are not responsible for their own problems (they are weak or sick) or for solutions (because they are incapable). The expert is called in to help find the solution, prescribe, counsel, suggest, and give orders that must be followed. In this case, the physician is clearly the expert. When patients are facing acute stress or living through acute problems that diminish their functioning, the medical model is very useful. It establishes that there is no blame on the part of the patient for having created the problem, thus relieving guilt. The physician takes responsibility for helping the patient to solve the problem through medication, counseling, or specific assignments that thereby relieve anxiety. For example, where the presenting complaint is recent onset rather than recurrent headaches as discussed above and a determination may be made that these headaches are caused by sinus infections, then a specific medical therapy (medical model) directed at eliminating the cause of these infections would be the most efficacious. In the absence of an infection, if the patient is reacting to a family crisis, the physician can prescribe specific stress-reduction techniques (behavioral aspirin) and expect compliance. This is also an application of the medical model. The physician takes responsibility for determining the therapeutic fix and allows the patient to be dependent. Other options open to the physician include making a family intervention or involving community agencies. The more acute the problem, the more important for the physician to take charge, at least temporarily. In an emergency situation, and emergency for the patient is a subjective state, authoritarian behavior helps to relieve stress.

By keeping these two models in mind and simply trying to determine if the problem is chronic (and needs an application of the compensatory model) or acute (and calls for the medical model), the physician can easily determine the more effective therapeutic role. In either case, the focus is on dealing with the problem. In general, the compensatory model fosters higher self-esteem in the patient, whereas the medical model satisfies dependency needs. Application of either helps the patient feel better and function better.

AIMING FOR SMALL WINS

In previous chapters, we have pointed out that feelings of powerlessness or demoralization bring the patient to a therapist.[7] It is feeling helpless in the face of threat that is devastating, physically and mentally.[8-10] In many cases, the overwhelming scope of problems faced by individuals, and for that matter, by society as a whole, predisposes people to feeling helpless, since there appears to be little that can be done to effect any kind of meaningful solution.

Weick[11] suggests that very often when we try to tackle overwhelming societal problems such as crime, traffic congestion, and pollution, the attempted large-scale solutions create new problems such as increased law enforcement removing needed funds from other services, multilane highways drawing more people away from mass transit, and the cost of pollution control raising taxes. However, the most detrimental aspect of the problem is that people's level of arousal gets raised without their having access to responses that will effectively impact on the situation. This is *stress*. People go on overload because of their perception of the severity and intensity of the problem while they feel hopeless to do anything about it.

The corrective strategy proposed by Weick is to focus on minor leverage points that enable people to engage in productive problem solving. In other words, people can act to make other people aware of the problem, organize rallies, write letters, wear red, white, and blue ribbons, get attention from the newspapers, and in that way feel as though they are accomplishing something. They are not just standing idly by, watching the world go to ruin.

Achieving small wins has the effect of reversing both overarousal and apathy, which result from feeling demoralized. When working with patients, the idea of focusing on small wins has practical, immediate, and surprisingly effective results. Anything that can be construed to lower the patient's level of psychological distress, that is, get them off *tilt*, is a therapeutic milestone. Getting patients to focus on some small changes that they can personally effect in their own behavior—changing a schedule slightly, carving out time for themselves, organizing a list, clearly asking for something they want, learning to express feelings without attacking or blaming, writing a letter, or perhaps only a postcard—can result in a small win. Doing one little task can provide a sense of having some power. There is less risk for patients when they tackle a problem in stages, since less is riding on each particular behavior. The outcome is more likely to be successful, and it will be less traumatic if it is not successful. The main idea is to make patients aware that what they do can make a difference. Weick says:

> Brief therapy is most successful when the client is persuaded to do just one thing differently that interdicts the pattern of attempted solutions up to that point. Extremely easy or extremely difficult goals are less compelling than are goals set closer to perceived capabilities. Learning tends to occur in small increments rather than in an all-or-none fashion.[12]

Small wins increase the chance of success, foster optimism, help people to refocus their energy productively, and restore belief in personal control. When belief is positive, firm actions are more likely to occur than when the person feels hesitant, doubtful, or cynical. The structure of the therapy grows out of the physician's belief in the patient's ability to effect small, meaningful changes.

ENGAGING THE PATIENT IN A PSYCHOTHERAPEUTIC CONTRACT

After physical examination and medical management decisions have been made, the physician returns to the psychosocial aspects. Determining the nature of the problem and giving an empathetic response constitute a psychotherapeutic intervention. As has been stated, it focuses the patient and legitimizes his or her feelings. The physician now suggests that regardless of the origin of the problem, little is gained by placing blame. Rather, it is important to determine what can be done to manage the situation by evaluating the available options. The physician becomes the patient's ally in dealing with the problem. One approach is to advise the patient to take some time to think about it and return the following week. If a patient is feeling overwhelmed and problems are numerous and complex, a contract, specifically a verbal understanding, is made for follow-up. It is helpful to specify that the physician will meet with the patient for a particular number of sessions.

In Chapter 9, we will discuss specific considerations that must be applied to patients presenting with certain problems or perhaps we should say certain problem patients: the hypochondriacal patient, the depressed or suicidal patient, and the grieving patient. All of these lend themselves to therapeutic intervention by the primary care physician, provided that the contract is made clear. The physician's role, commitment, and limitations must be clearly spelled out. The patient's responsibilities must also be stated, acknowledged, and documented in the chart. Any time that the physician feels overwhelmed by the extent of the patient's problems, a psychiatric consult or referral is indicated. Patients to be referred include psychotic, addicted, or violent patients or any whose condition makes the physician feel uncomfortable. When referring a patient, there is an understanding that the physician will continue to be involved with the patient and continue to provide ongoing medical care.

Example: The Suicidal Patient

Suicidal patients should be seen as experiencing excruciating psychological pain. They are able to see only *one* potential for turning off the pain, that is, turning themselves off. The doctor imparts confidence that there are less drastic measures for relief than *permanently* destroying one's self. Suicide is a permanent solution to what may turn out to be a temporary problem. The doctor elicits a promise that the patient will discuss options and postpone doing anything that cannot be changed. A specific appointment is made and the patient is expected to honor this commitment. Hope is rekindled. Respect and caring are also communicated.

Please note that it is important to ascertain whether the patient has made actual plans. If there is a realistic danger of self-destructive behavior, the patient may have to be hospitalized, although this may be avoided if there is a support person available to stay with the patient through the acute phase of the patient's despondency. More will be said about this later.

DETERMINING THE NUMBER OF SESSIONS

We know from crisis theory, as described by Gerald Caplan,[4] that a situational crisis is usually resolved in six to eight weeks. As discussed in Chapter 2, crisis is a time of great stress, meaning that people are having to adjust to a particular acute or anticipated change. During a period of crisis, people function less efficiently than when they feel secure and have a sense of well-being. People under stress regress to more primitive modes of behavior, have a narrower view, a harder time with problem solving and cannot see the possible options.[11] The physician's role in providing support engages the person's sense of well-being and provides the patient with an ally in dealing with the problem.

In making a contract for follow-up, the physician commits to following the patient through the time of greatest stress. From crisis theory, it is obvious that six or eight weeks provide a reasonable expectation of problem resolution. The physician arranges to see the patient regularly during that time. Once a week is appropriate if the problem is serious. Once every other week is sufficient if the patient is less overwhelmed. If the patient is feeling totally unstrung, twice a week may be necessary during the acute phase of the crisis.

By agreeing to see the patient regularly and briefly for a specified number of sessions, a message is conveyed that the problem is solvable and that the physician expects resolution to come within a reasonable period of time. Conveying this message is part of the therapeutic intervention. Hope is engaged since patients recognize that the physician sees factors that work against their feelings of despair. Perhaps the problem is manageable after all. Patients regain a sense of worth that is conveyed by the physician wanting to engage with the patient in the resolution of this problem. It is a consistent message. The physician is not only saying that the patient is worthy and deserving, but is making a specific commitment to work with the patient. The fact that the physician places no blame but suggests that the problem needs to be resolved is practical. Contracting to help the patient resolve the problem is one of the most affirming and therapeutic messages that can be conveyed. The patient has a partner and feels less overwhelmed by the problem and less isolated. Often, the patient feels so much better that the number of sessions can be reduced.

Example: The Grieving Patient

Work with the grieving patient can usually be accomplished in six or eight sessions. When working with a bereaved patient or discovering a situation of unresolved grief during a routine inquiry, it is important that the physician explain the need for working through feelings related to significant relationships that have been terminated through death or other circumstances. The physician then can refer the patient or contract with the patient for a brief period of therapy. The therapy will focus primarily on reviewing the significant aspects of the terminated relationship, coming to terms with the good and bad aspects, and then letting go.

THE EFFICACY OF TIME

The therapy provided by the physician consists of providing a special time and environment where the patient can reassess his or her options. The patient has a chance to reexamine responses to situations, chart new goals, and get a more positive sense of competence. The doctor helps the patient focus on one particular problem and suggests that the process can then be replicated by the patient. The time constraint is useful because it works against overloading the patient and adding to the confusion. The doctor conveys optimism that problems can be resolved one at a time. The physician is there to help the patient work through the problems. By returning to patients the sense of having some potential for affecting the course of their lives and making their own decisions and choices, the physician is acting in a most effective psychotherapeutic manner. In addition, by incorporating this approach with each patient and on every encounter, the physician builds efficiency into his or her practice. A little energy invested in this process on each visit can help foster the image of the physician as an empathetic and involved figure. This enables the physician to handle patients' problems in an effective and timely fashion, often before they assume overwhelming proportions.

SUMMARY

It is essential to include the psychotherapeutic intervention into a fifteen minute office visit. The therapy grows out of the physician-patient relationship. The acronym BATHE summarizes the approach to handling the context of the visit. B stands for background: "What is going on?" A stands for affect: "How do you feel about it?" T stands for trouble: "What about it bothers you most?" H stands for handling: "How are you dealing with that?" E stands for empathy: "That must be very difficult for you." By BATHEing the patient early in the visit, an effective and efficient psychotherapeutic intervention is structured into every patient encounter. Multiple problems can be handled by sequentially applying this simple technique. Medication can be used as an adjunct to psychotherapy.

The *compensatory model* is best for chronic problems while the *medical model* is more supportive in acute situations. Small wins, which help the patient experience success, are effective in promoting change through establishing confidence and by combating the sense of being overwhelmed.

The physician engages the patient in therapy by establishing a contract to follow the psychosocial context of the patient's life. Suicidal patients may be treated if seen as considering a permanent solution for a temporary problem. When they are encouraged to leave their options open, hope can be rekindled.

Crises can generally be resolved within six or eight weeks, which is also a good estimate for dealing with grief reactions. The same time constraint inherent in the brief session is useful because it avoids overloading the patient. The physician's optimism and focus on one problem at a time is effective.

REFERENCES

1. Vaillant, G. E. *Adaptation to Life*. Boston: Little, Brown, 1977.
2. Weed, L. L. *Medical Records, Medical Education, and Patient Care*. Cleveland: The Press of Case Western Reserve, 1969.
3. Kallman, H. and Stuart, M. R. BATH—A simple mnemonic to integrate psychosocial data into a soaped chart. Unpublished manuscript. 1980.
4. Caplan, G. *Principles of Preventive Psychiatry*. New York: Basic Books, 1964.
5. Weissman, M. M. The psychological treatment of depression: Evidence for the efficacy of psychotherapy alone in comparison with and in combination with pharmacotherapy. *Archives of General Psychiatry*, 1979, *36*, 1261–1269.
6. Brickman, P., Rabinowitz, V. C., Karuza, J., Jr., et al. Models of helping and coping. *American Psychologist*, 1982, *37*, 368–384.
7. Frank, J. D. Psychotherapy: The restoration of morale. *American Journal of Psychiatry*, 1974, *131*, 271–274.
8. Spilken, A. Z. and Jacobs M. A. Prediction of illness behaviors from measures of life crisis, manifest distress and maladaptive coping. *Psychosomatic Medicine*, 1971, *33*, 251–264.
9. Cox, T. and MacKay, C. Psychosocial factors and psychophysiological mechanisms in the aetiology and development of cancer. *Social Science and Medicine*, 381–396.
10. Levy, S. M., Herberman, R. B., et al. Prognostic risk assessment in primary breast cancer by behavioral and immunological parameters. *Health Psychology*, 1985, *4*, 99–113.
11. Weick, K. E. Small Wins: Redefining the scale of social problems. *American Psychologist*, 1984, *39*, 40–49.
12. Op. cit., p. 45.

Rationale and Techniques for Fifteen Minute Therapy

7

Patients generally assume that their physicians are technically competent to diagnose and treat disease. The physician's interest in the patient as an individual and his or her demonstrated warmth and support, particularly in the presence of debilitating, painful, or frightening symptoms, are an added bonus.

McWhinney[1] has pointed out that physicians are much more adept at applying the biological and physical sciences to the practice of medicine than they are in utilizing knowledge from the behavioral sciences. Every patient with an organic illness also "exhibits some form of behavior." It is important for the physician to become aware of this behavior, as well as the social context of the patient's symptoms. Even where psychiatric symptoms are the chief complaint, McWhinney feels that most of the emotional disorders in general medical practice fall into the category of "problems of living," that is, the natural anxiety of people who are responding to perceived threats to their health or wellbeing. Although, as previously pointed out, a patient's response to illness is determined by many factors, including genetic makeup, early history, previous experience with illness, current life situation, and aspirations for the future, McWhinney points out that of all these factors, the current life situation is the most amenable to alteration by the physician. For this reason, it is critical that the physician routinely ask all patients about what is going on in their lives.

ROUTINE INQUIRIES ABOUT CURRENT LIFE SITUATION

The situational context of the patient's life helps the physician understand the significance of the patient's symptomatology.

Sickness Is Often Triggered by Psychological or Social Stress

The list of psychological factors that may precipitate illness is extensive. McWhinney has devised a taxonomy that identifies seven general areas:

1. Loss—either personal, such as bereavement or divorce, or loss of something valued, such as a home, position, or object.
2. Conflict—interpersonal or intrapersonal, having to do with conflicting internal demands.
3. Change—either triggered by life cycle events or a geographical one.
4. Maladjustment—interpersonal problems not having to do with acute conflicts; failure to adjust to occupational or home demands.
5. Other stresses, acute or chronic.
6. General isolation.
7. Failure or frustrated expectations.

We would add to this list:

8. Any anniversary of a significant loss or traumatic event.[2,3]

These are the types of situations that impact on the health of the patient. They are also the situations that lower the patient's threshold of tolerance for the discomfort of symptoms or the threshold for anxiety about symptoms. Since patients are often not aware of this relationship, they are very relieved when the physician helps them to make this connection.

Stress Often Exacerbates Chronic Conditions

A diabetic may have been well controlled for years and suddenly presents in the office because routine dipstick testing revealed spilling of sugar. Perhaps the most important question that the physician can ask is, "What is going on in your life?" It may turn out that the patient is afraid of getting fired, his wife is threatening to leave him, a teenage daughter has an older boyfriend who is making sexual demands on her, or perhaps there are financial problems related to college costs for children. These or any other situational stress can easily precipitate an exacerbation of the diabetic symptomatology and can best be managed with a psychological rather than chemical intervention.

The Physician's Interest Is Supportive

The physician's interest in the patient is demonstrated by the inquiry about the social context of the patient's problem. In this way, the physician demonstrates warmth and caring and affirms the individuality and importance of the patient. The patient has to make sense out of the physician's behavior. There are only two possible explanations for the physician's show of interest. One is that the physician is a warm and caring person, which makes the patient feel safe and in good hands. The other explanation is that the patient is a worthwhile person who has some significance for the physician. This also makes the patient feel good. In either case, the patient will feel supported and hence be able to tolerate symptoms better.[4]

When physicians routinely inquire into the circumstances of a patient's life, the patient becomes aware of the physical-psychological interaction. Understanding the effects of stress on the physical responses of the body helps to make the patient feel more in control and, therefore, less anxious. Becoming aware of the effects of stress is a prerequisite for learning to manage it. If we are not aware that we are becoming tense, then there is no behavioral cue for applying relaxation techniques, be they physical or cognitive. Understanding the significance of an anniversary and its potential for precipitating illness and the high correlation of anniversaries with accidents[2,3] can keep patients from overreacting, turning acute events into chronic conditions, and setting unrealistic expectations for themselves.

A patient will almost sheepishly present with chest pain on the anniversary of his father's heart attack, saying, "I know it's probably psychosomatic, Doc, but check it out anyway and relieve my anxiety. Every year at this time, I seem to develop these symptoms." After ruling out the acute condition, it would be appropriate to encourage the patient to reassess his relationship with his father. If he has not completely dealt with his grief, it is important for him to focus on both the good and bad memories of his youth and come to terms with the remaining ambivalent feelings.

DEALING WITH PATIENT'S REACTIONS

Once the physician has determined the context of the visit in terms of what is going on in the patient's life, it is important to inquire about the patient's emotional reaction. "How do you feel about that?" is the most efficient question to ask. Not, "Why do you think this is happening?" or "What does your wife think about it?" The point is to get the patient to make an affective response. "How do you feel about it?"

usually elicits a response that starts with "I feel. . . . " If the patient starts to offer other information, it is important for the physician to interrupt and to persist, "Yes, I understand, but how do you *feel* about the situation?" We would caution practitioners not to get caught up in the details of the patient's situation. Finding out who said what to whom has no therapeutic significance. We are interested in having the patient label and express feelings so that we can empathize and then attempt to focus the patient on the problem-solving strategy. Just having the patient acknowledge "I am angry," or, "I am sad," or, "I feel rejected," "scared," "powerless," "overwhelmed," or "totally confused," are all useful. Most people react automatically or semiautomatically to most of the events in their lives, without much conscious awareness or thought about what they are feeling. Just by focusing their attention by an act of will we have broken the pattern. If feelings are experienced and acknowledged, they may not need to become psychosomatic symptoms.

When the physician inquires about how the patient is feeling about a specific situation, the physician changes the focus from what is happening to how the patient is reacting. This puts the emphasis on the patient and clearly demonstrates the physician's concern about the patient. The physician is extending an invitation to get at the root of what is actually troubling the patient. By next inquiring about the significance of the event, the physician in a subtle way implies that the interpretation about what is troubling the patient is not necessarily obvious. This simple device may prepare the patient to see the situation as less catastrophic or at least to recognize the need to develop potential solutions. The physician assumes no meaning or judgment, thereby fulfilling Rogers's[5] caveat for providing nonjudgmental acceptance.

As part of the initial inquiry, the physician now has a choice. One option is to ask the patient how the situation is being handled and then responding empathetically. The other choice is first to acknowledge that the situation must be difficult and then to ask how the patient might handle it.

Many physicians schedule patients with emotional problems for the end of the day in order to leave time to explore the situation fully. We strongly recommend against this practice, since it involves too much of an investment on the part of the physician and may not necessarily result in increased benefits for the patient. Since it has generally been established that, given a positive doctor-patient relationship, all psychotherapeutic techniques work equally well,[6-8] we strongly urge primary care physicians to practice and overlearn (do them so often that

Rationale and Techniques of Therapy

they become automatic) the techniques we are describing, since they are effective and do not take much time.

When a physician invites a patient to talk without structuring the interview, it is possible that the patient will gain many benefits, but the process is quite random. Our experience is that patients will complain incessantly and repeatedly about the behavior of other people and circumstances that cannot be changed, thereby reinforcing their limited interpretation of their reality. Allowing patients to go on and on about these matters is countertherapeutic, tries the patience of the physician, and sets up unreasonable expectations on the part of the patient regarding the amount of time the physician has available. Not only that, we often find that the longer the patient talks, the more upset he or she gets. By giving the patient valuable time and listening attentively to unchanging complaints, the physician may support the patient's distorted perceptions. Ultimately, the physician may decide that it is not worth trying to treat the psychological aspects of a patient's problems.

Perhaps, over time, the patient's self-esteem may be enhanced by the attention of the accepting physician. This is the assumption behind Rogers's[5] client-centered therapy. However, we feel strongly that it is much more economical in terms of time and emotional energy to make one or two interventions that directly challenge, and, therefore, potentially change the patient's assumptive world view or behavior, rather than just letting the patient talk.

> A 55-year-old woman comes to the office complaining of fatigue. She says that she has been tired for weeks. She has had no physical exam for years. There is no significant medical history. Asked about what is going on in her life, she says that both she and her husband work full time, she is also a homemaker, and takes care of her 17-year-old son, who is legally blind, but has just been accepted into college. She looks frightened, depressed, and essentially closed. Asked how she feels about what is going on, she only volunteers that she is tired. The physical exam is unremarkable, blood and urine tests and a pelvic exam all are normal. The physician thinks perhaps the patient might be depressed. He asks, "Do you have any idea what you might be depressed about?" The patient replies, "I work a 40-hour week. Keep my own house. Cook dinner every night. I have a nice husband who would be happy with a bologna sandwich, but wouldn't make it for himself. Oh yes, my sister cares for our 90-year-old father. I go over there every Saturday to help

out. I really wish she'd put him in a nursing home, but I feel guilty when I think that, and my sister won't hear of it."

The physician responds that he thinks that that is a very reasonable way to feel. The patient sighs. She looks relieved and volunteers that she has done nothing for herself in recent times. The physician suggests that she make just one small change. The patient smiles, "I can do that. Thank you so much, Doctor, I feel so much better."

As we have said previously, psychological intervention consists of interrupting fixed patterns of behavior by focusing attention either on the behavior or away from it, by distracting the person and/or focusing on other options. By BATHEing the patient, we are focusing on the feelings and the behavior of the patient and setting the stage for change.

Often, the initial sequence is all that is required in the way of psychological support. It is only in those patients where the situational stress is currently unmanageable that the physician should engage the patient in a specific therapeutic contract.

Dealing with Unexpected Reactions During the Interview

Often as part of taking a history, a routine question about previous hospitalizations, family illness, or previous geographical moves may elicit a strong emotional reaction in a patient, that is, trigger painful memories. The physician may be at a loss whether to ignore, soothe, or deeply explore the reaction. BATHEing provides a constructive alternative.

> A young woman presented in the office complaining of a sore throat. Initial inquiry was unremarkable. However, when asked if there was any family history of rheumatic fever, she suddenly started to cry and recalled that while she was in high school she had been put to bed for several months because of rheumatic fever. The physician was first taken aback and hesitant to get into an old painful experience. However, since something had to be done, the physician decided to apply the BATHE technique. The physician inquired about the *background*: "You were in high school, about what grade?"
>
> "I was just starting my senior year."
>
> Going right to *affect*, the physician inquired, "And they put you on complete bed rest, how did you feel about that?"

The patient replied, "I felt so isolated and out of it."

The physician did not allow herself to explore these feelings further but inquired directly about *trouble*: "What about the situation troubled you the most?"

"I was afraid that I would not graduate with my class."

"How did you *handle* that?" was the final question.

"Well, there wasn't much I could do. I had to go to summer school. It was awful."

The empathetic response followed. "I can see that that was a very difficult time for you. Tell me, any other serious illnesses?"

The patient responded, "No." Then after a pause, "You know, at this point it really doesn't make any difference. As a matter of fact, now that I think of it, I think I did better in college because I worked for a year first."

The physician responded. "I'm glad. Now I'd like to examine you and make sure that everything else is OK."

FOCUSING ON OPTIONS

In dealing with a patient's situational stress, it is crucial that the physician not take responsibility for solving the patient's problems. In the *House of God*,[9] a biting satire about medical education, one of the primary truths, RULE FOUR, clearly states "The patient is the one with the disease." If the patient is the one with the disease or the problem, the patient has a right to decide what, if anything, should be done about it. The physician has the opportunity to intervene in the process simply by making the patient aware of the options and encouraging the patient to make an informed choice about what will be done. There are three strategies that the physician may choose to present to the patient: looking at the consequences, applying tincture of time, and choosing not to choose.

Looking at Consequences

The physician can encourage the patient to think about and/or list several possible courses of behavior and to sort out the consequences inherent in these choices. A good structure is to ask the patient to specify what the best and worst possible outcomes might be. Patients who are very angry often talk about wanting to kill the offending party. Rather than responding, "You don't mean that!" (yes, they do, at least for the moment), or, "You can't do that!" (yes, they can, it's not a good idea, but it is possible), the effective reply is, "I can understand that you would feel that way, but that does not sound like a very practical option when you consider the consequences. Let's talk again next week, and see what you might do that's more constructive." The implication here is that the feeling is legitimate (it is!) but that once the patient thinks about it, other behavioral choices will appear and the decision about what to do can be deferred at least until the following week.

Applying Tincture of Time

It is often true that the more important a decision is, the less information we have to base it on and the less time we take to make it. We put a deposit on a desirable house after one or two brief visits because if we don't act immediately, someone else is likely to snap it up. Then we spend hours choosing among shades of paint or wallpaper patterns.

Often a patient who is reacting emotionally to an event may feel impelled to make a decision. Having learned of her husband's unfaithfulness, a wife may feel either she must leave him immediately or have an affair herself. The physician encourages the patient to take time to sort out the feelings. Reacting to an acute loss involves an increased intensity of pain. The physician offers support and schedules an appointment to talk again. The implication is that tincture of time will provide relief.

Choosing Not to Choose

In a case where all apparent choices are unacceptable and the patient does not want to choose the lesser of the evils, the physician can also instruct the patient that for the moment at least the best course of action may be to do nothing. Sometimes all the important information is not available to make an intelligent choice. "What is the worst thing that can happen if you don't make a decision about this?" To choose not to choose is an option that many people never consider. Psychological pain is something that must be felt but often does not require a behavioral response. Often there is no need to act, especially if the pain is induced by the actions of another person over whom we have no control. In many cases, breaking patterns by not acting in response to provocation by another shifts the balance of power.

THE EFFECTS OF SYMBOLISM

One of the more fascinating aspects of practicing primary care medicine is the opportunity to interact meaningfully with a variety of people. The specialist who treats limited organ systems is only excited by unusual manifestations of disease and opportunities to diagnose rare cases. The primary care physician can be endlessly impressed by the different reactions that individuals have to the same circumstances. The particular meaning that each of us attributes to an event determines our reaction rather than the event proper. In every case where a person appears to be overreacting to a particular situation, we can assume that there is a symbolic meaning to that circumstance that is triggering the patient's reaction.

> Mr. Harris, a 28-year-old white male, presented in the emergency room with chest pain and difficulty breathing of sudden onset. He had no risk factors for heart disease and examination, electrocardiogram, and enzyme studies were totally normal. The physician was aware that Mrs. Harris was due to deliver their first child momentarily and that the couple was extremely happy about the prospect of becoming parents. Arrangements were complete and Mr. Harris had planned to stay with his wife during the delivery.
> After reassuring the patient about the condition of his heart, the doctor inquired about what was currently happening. She was informed that the obstetrician had just told the couple that the baby was in breach position and that he had decided to do a cesarean section. At this point the patient started to cry. He revealed that he himself had been a breach delivery and that his mother had died in childbirth. He was sure that his wife would not survive. He had so wanted to be present at the birth but now could not face the prospect.
> The physician was able to reassure him about the improvement in obstetrical procedures over the past 28 years and the relatively low risk associated with breach presentation when delivered by cesarean section. However, the physician did point out that it was perfectly OK to be concerned and scared. The patient was then able to connect his severe reaction to his own tragic birth circumstances rather than the current situation. The physician

suggested that perhaps the patient needed to bring a support person to the hospital for himself. The following week, a proud father, gowned and masked, held his wife's hand in the operating room and watched his son take his first breath.

When helping the patient tie particular reactions to their historical roots, the physician implies that the patient now can break the pattern of response and reassess the significance of particular situations in the here and now. You may have a particular intolerance to people's loud arguing because when you were a child your parents fought bitterly. Listening to them, you felt helpless and frightened because your security was threatened. Whenever you hear people arguing, you feel helpless and frightened just as you did then. If a physician were to ask you gently, "Are you really helpless now? As an adult, is your security threatened?", you would become aware of the change in your circumstances and learn to monitor your reaction to loud arguments and, thereby, affect a change.

The physician's brief inquiry about the historical roots of an event can have a profound effect on a patient's self-esteem, sense of control, feelings of acceptability, and assumptive world view. It is not necessary to explore the circumstances, distortions, or details in depth. Simply point out to the patient that there appears to be an inconsistency in the severity of the reaction in relation to the apparent face value of the event. Patients can be asked to write an autobiography, keep a journal of current reactions, or compare memories with various living relatives in order to sort out the origins of some of their troubling interpersonal reactions. Often this will promote constructive dialogue with significant persons in the patient's life. The important factor here is always that it is the patient who must understand and ultimately change reactions. The physician's understanding by and of itself accomplishes absolutely nothing. As Shem[9] has said, "The patient is the one with the disease." The patient is the one who must make the connections and change the responses.

FOCUSING THE PATIENT IN THE PRESENT

In previous sections, we have discussed the significance of the origins of various clinical manifestations of reactions to current life stress. When engaging a patient psychotherapeutically in the fifteen minute hour, we propose that it is crucial for the physician to stress that although the historical significance for the patient is enlightening, the past is past, and all we have to deal with is the here and now. Dwelling on past hurts is not useful: "Do you still resent your brother now, because your mother always favored him when you were kids? Really?" "Gee, I guess I do." "My guess is that your mother did the very best that she could. What would it take for you to forgive her?" The reality is that when we hold on to grudges or nurse our resentments, our bodies pay a price. We make ourselves miserable and do not actually affect the people that we are angry with.

Just as there is no benefit to obsessing about past hurts, assumptions made about the future are usually wrong and destructive. When a patient generalizes from a current unfavorable situation to speculate about a bleak outlook, the physician needs to challenge this distortion, for example: "I understand that your husband has left you, and that you feel very hurt. However, it is not legitimate to assume that no one will *ever* love you again." "Yes, it is very painful to have your article rejected by the *AAI Journal*. You worked very hard on it and were sure it would be accepted. However, that does not mean that *no one* will ever publish it." "You are feeling very unhappy right now, that does not mean that you will never be happy again." When a patient says, "I know that such and such will happen because it always has," it is important to correct him or her and restate, "You *assume* that such and such will happen. What is it that you could possibly do to change that?"

It is important to encourage the patient to take one day at a time. If the patient is in extreme pain, it may be necessary to suggest taking it *five minutes* at a time. Then the patient is to acknowledge that accomplishment to him- or herself. Patients should also be cautioned that wallowing in their pain is not constructive. If they really feel the need to wallow occasionally, they may be given permission to do so, providing they limit wallowing to five minute sessions. Patients really respond quite well to these kinds of instructions. It puts their pain into context and gives them a sense of control.

These edicts, stated with the authority of the physician, and with the attributed social power inherent in the role, may help the patient reassess the resources that are available for dealing with current problems. The physician's encouragement to reassess reality in the here and now, rather than dwelling on the past which cannot be changed, or the future, which we cannot accurately predict, is very productive. Our experience is that patients are usually depressed about the past and anxious about the future. If we can focus them in the present and engage them in problem solving rather than fight/flight reactions, they respond incredibly well.

THREE-STEP PROBLEM SOLVING

In this volume we have promoted several cookbook approaches to therapy because they provide a simple structure to trigger physicians efforts to help patients. In Chapter 4 we introduced the PLISSIT structure to determine levels of intervention including simple permission giving, limited information, specific suggestions, and finally a contract for intensive therapy. In Chapter 6 and the current chapter, we have repeatedly preached about the benefits of BATHEing the patient to determine and manage the situational context of the patient visit. Now we propose a three-step sequence of questions to apply to any disturbing situation. These questions are:

1. What am I feeling?
2. What do I want?
3. What can I do about it?

This is a useful framework for physicians to apply to their own reactions, as will be discussed in Chapter 9. For the present, let us focus back on the patient. The series of questions now becomes:

1. What are you feeling? (Label the actual feeling.)
2. What do you want? (Be specific.)
3. What can *you* do about it? (Focus on what you can control.)

For example, patient X is complaining about how his daughter's attitude disturbs him. The physician asks, "What are you feeling?" The patient may try to continue ranting about his daughter's behavior and how she should be. He says they fight all the time and he screams at her. The physician persists, "What do you feel in that situation?" or "How do you *feel* about that?" It may turn out that the patient feels angry, hurt, frightened, excluded, disappointed, devalued, disgusted, or some other unpleasant sensation, depending on the meaning of his daughter's attitude for him.

At this point the physician acknowledges that feeling and asks, "What do you want?" At first the patient will respond that he doesn't want to be in this situation. The physician persists, "What do *you* want?" The reply is, "I want her to change her behavior." (Sometimes patients say they don't really know, in which case the physician can encourage them to think about that and come back to talk more.)

The final question, "What can you do about that? I understand that fighting with her has not been helpful." The patient may decide that he can reward appropriate behavior, make a contract, discuss it quietly, and present the situation to his daughter as a problem to be solved. Sometimes there is nothing that can be done. In this case, what the patient feels about the situation changes to appropriate sadness. It is hard to accept the fact that we cannot control other people's attitudes and behavior.

In any case, this three-step process labels feelings, clarifies what the patient wants, and points to a direction for achieving these goals. It is economical in time and direct in therapeutic value, since it encourages new ways of thinking and behaving and discourages the passive role. It is also teaching a strategy to the patient that can be applied to any number of situations.

PHYSICIAN SUPPORT PUTS THE PATIENT IN CONTROL

We have said that the feeling of being overwhelmed is the trigger for patients' help-seeking behavior. By engaging the patients as we have suggested, patients become aware of having some control over the circumstances of their lives. Since the relationship with the physician is an ongoing one, patients feel that they have a partner and, therefore, feel less isolated. Someone cares and wants to follow their progress. If feelings of abandonment help to trigger unpleasant reactions, now there is an assurance of ongoing support that will continue to be available over time.

The second important factor to be considered concerns the patient's reaction to the physician's expectation that the patient is capable of handling the situation. The physician has indicated that the patient has choices, the patient's reactions are legitimate, and there are actions available to the patient that will improve the current situation. If the patient is able to hear and accept these messages, it will change how the patient feels about the particular circumstances. Certainly, the patient is no longer helpless and no longer feels hopeless. This may even make the situation appear less hopeless and ultimately improve it.

A constructive attitude toward the physician's intervention will engage a positive cycle. Since the patient will feel less overwhelmed, the patient will resume normal and more effective functioning. The more mature coping mechanisms will be engaged. The patient's view of the situation will broaden and novel stimuli will be experienced and processed. The patient will be able to solve problems more effectively and have a sense of being more in control. He or she can then be expected to communicate more clearly and directly to let others know what is needed. This improved functioning will be reinforced by more successful efforts at attaining desired outcomes.

Focusing on Strengths

Every person or situation has good and bad potential. It is definitely more therapeutic to focus on positive aspects of a situation and on the positive qualities of a person. A glass that is half full is to be preferred over one that is half empty. There is strong evidence to support the need to be optimistic and speak in positive terms. A recent study showed that patients react much more favorably to being told that there is a 68 percent survival rate than that there is a 32 percent mortality rate.[10] We can speculate that in the first instance a patient focuses on the word survival and in the second only mortality is heard. The numbers are strongly discounted. In every case we are seeing patients who have clearly demonstrated their ability to survive, since if they had not, we would not be seeing them in our office at this time. If is important to focus on the strengths that have brought them this far.

The Patient Is Responsible

The support of the physician is available but must be asked for. The patient is held responsible for applying strategies that have been discussed and investigating various options. This is in accordance with the compensatory model. The patient is encouraged to stay in the here and now and to take things one day at a time. There is an understanding that the situation will be discussed further at the next visit. The time interval is clearly specified: "I want to see you next week and we will talk more."

The New Scoring System

A final word about evaluating the patients' response. We have invented an innovative scoring system for keeping track of new behavior. It is designed to focus only on positive changes and discount lapses. Since we know that under stress people regress and are not easily able to apply most recently learned behavior,[11] patients must be encouraged to keep track of every time they engage in new behavior. We are not interested in recording failures (too many patients are stuck in the failure image), only instances of success. They are to give themselves credit (two points) when they become aware of reacting, thinking, behaving, planning, or doing anything in a new way, that is, changing old patterns.

Since it is hard to act in new ways or apply new behavioral techniques, doing it and recognizing it deserve two points. It is essential to caution patients not to get angry or abusive with themselves when they become aware that they are reacting in old ways. On the contrary, they get credit just for the recognition. It is normal and to be expected that under stress patients will often react in automatic old ways. That is how they have done it for years. It is overlearned and has become a habit. Habits are hard to break. The first step to changing behavior that has become habitual is to start to become aware of it as it is happening. That is the reason that we suggest that patients give themselves credit (one point) every time they catch themselves doing something the old way. Becoming conscious of the behavior as it is occurring and starting to self-monitor are prerequisites for making lasting changes. By suggesting that the patient is doing something good, even when the patient is acting in the usual old way, we are helping the patient break the destructive cycle of feeling helpless and then abusing the self for feeling helpless. A positive change has been induced. In the next chapter we will be looking at the content of the fifteen minute therapy session and will introduce some further strategies and suggestions.

SUMMARY

Since illness or accidents exacerbate chronic conditions, and sickness is often triggered by psychosocial stress, the physician should routinely ask all patients what is going on in their lives. The physician's interest indicates caring about the whole person. By making the inquiry routine, patients are educated to become aware of the interaction between their physical and psychological well-being.

If a patient is upset about the present situation, the physician extends an invitation to talk. The physician tries to establish the significance of the event for the patient and accepts the patient's feelings. When a patient unexpectedly reacts emotionally during the course of an interview, the physician briefly explores the issue by BATHEing the patient. In difficult situations, the physician suggests that there might be options, invites the patient to consider consequences related to different choices, and suggests that applying "tincture of time" or deciding not to decide are viable options.

The physician makes the patient aware that events have a symbolic significance that is different for all people, that certain feelings are triggered by old memories, and that self-esteem, the sense of control, and the sense of being lovable are all affected by the patient's interpretation of certain historical events. The physician points out that these old interpretations can then affect current relationships.

The patient is then focused in the present. The physician stresses that the past is past and all we have to deal with is the here and now. Dwelling on past hurts is not useful and assumptions made about the future are usually wrong. It is important not to generalize and to take life one day at a time. Under extreme circumstances, taking life five minutes at a time may be better. Patients generally feel guilty about the past and anxious about the future so focusing in the present and engaging in active problem solving is therapeutic.

A three-step approach to problem solving involves asking what the patient is feeling, what the patient wants, and what the patient can do to maximize getting what he or she wants. The physician's support makes the patient feel more in control. The patient has a partner. The physician indicates confidence in the patient's ability to handle things. The patient feels less overwhelmed and resumes functioning in a healthier mode.

The physician focuses on the patient's strength, acknowledges that the patient has survived similar situations, that support is available and can be asked for, and that the situation will be discussed further at the next visit. A scoring system that only records successes is instigated to reinforce new and more productive behavior.

REFERENCES

1. McWhinney, I. R. Beyong diagnosis: An approach to the integration of behavioral science and clinical medicine. *New England Journal of Medicine*, 1972, *287*, 384-387.

2. Bornstein, P. E. and Clayton, P. J. The anniversary reaction. *Diseases of the Nervous System*, 1972, *33*, 470-472.

3. Cavenar, J. O. Jr., Nash, J. I., and Maltbie, A. A. Anniversary reactions presenting as physical complaints. *The Journal of Clinical Psychiatry*, 1978, 369-374.

4. Cassel, J. Psychosocial processes and "stress": Theoretical formulation. *International Journal of Health Services*, 1974, *4*, 471-482.

5. Rogers, C. R. The necessary and sufficient conditions of therapeutic personality change. *Journal of Consulting Psychology*, 1957, *21*, 95-103.

6. Jonas, A. D. and Jonas D. F. Just how does psychological intervention modify behavior? *Medical Times*, 1979, *107*, 16d(106)-24d(106).

7. Agras, W. S. The behavioral treatment of somatic disorders. In Gentry, W. D., ed., *Handbook of Behavioral Medicine*. New York: Guilford Press, 1984.

8. Frank, J. D. Therapeutic components. In Myers, J. M., ed., *Cures by Psychotherapy: What Effects Change?* New York: Praeger, 1984.

9. Shem, S. *The House of God*. New York: Dell, 1979.

10. McNeil, B. J, Pauker, S. G., Sox, H. C., and Tversky, A. On the elicitation of preferences for alternative therapies. *New England Journal of Medicine*, 1981, *306*, 1259-1262.

11. Cohen, S. Aftereffects of stress on human performance and social behavior: A review of research and theory. *Psychological Bulletin*, 1980, *88*, 82-108.

8
Contents of the Fifteen Minute Therapy Session

We have now reached a point where we are addressing what transpires between the physician and the patient in the sessions that are devoted primarily to counseling or psychotherapy, whichever term is preferred. Our bias is to use the term psychotherapy because we are actually treating the patient, trying to promote a change in emotional or cognitive reactions. We hope that this will be a lasting change in approach or direction toward others or themselves, a change in their assumptive world view. Counseling suggests a process of giving advice related to a particular situation. It fosters dependency and implies that the physician has more insight into the situation than the patient does. We would like to propose a compromise, that the physician do therapy but call it counseling.

Let us assume that the physician recognizes that the process of the interaction with the patient that transpires in the fifteen minute session is psychotherapy—it can still be presented to the patient as counseling, which may make the patient more comfortable. In this way everyone will be satisfied. We do urge the physician to interact with the patient with awareness that the psychotherapeutic process implies facilitating change in the patient's assumptions about the world and how the world can be accessed to provide more generously for the patient's needs. The physician aims to promote the patient's sense of personal competence and connection to other people. The physician also tries to act in a manner and point out strategies that will help to foster the patient's sense that the world is a reasonably reliable place. This is intended to help to develop the patient's sense of coherence, the factor cited as most significant in promoting health.[1] Basically, the physician is using a variety of techniques to help the patient adapt to the environment in ways that will promote mental and physical health. Let us look at how all this can be effectively incorporated into a fifteen minute therapy session.

OPENING INQUIRY

It is important to start every session with an open question and let the patient talk about whatever he or she has been planning to say, thinking about, or finds most important to discuss at this time.

"How are things going?" "Tell me how you've been doing?" "What sort of things have you been thinking about since last week?" "Tell me how you've been feeling, and what's been going on." Any of these are good for openers. It is important to let the patient talk without interrupting for about two or three minutes. This gives the patient the opportunity to reflect on what seems to be most important at the time. After listening for about three minutes, it is important to summarize what the patient has said in order to let the patient know that the physician has been really listening.

If the patient has not focused on what has transpired in the time since the previous visit, then it is necessary to focus on the current situation and shortcut elaborate background material by asking a question such as "What has happened since I saw you last?" Next the physician may assess the patient's affect and phrase the inquiry by reflecting, "You look less tense, how do you feel about what's been going on?", or, "How have you been feeling since I saw you last?"

Next, it is good to ask, "What is the worst thing that has happened since last time?", or, "What has bothered you the most?" It may be useful to explore what about the situation made it bothersome. It is the symbolic meaning of the event for the patient that is important. Finally, the physician should ask how the patient feels about how things were handled.

It is good to focus on a success by saying, for example, "Tell me about one thing that you handled well or that you feel good about" or, "What is the best thing that has happened since I saw you?" The small wins and the sense of mastery that grows with effecting small wins is so very important.

The sequence of these questions is deliberate. It focuses the patient in the present and helps the patient identify and express feelings. It develops an awareness in the patient that during each time period there are both good and bad things that happen and choices that the patient makes in responding to them. These techniques are generic to the process of therapy. We are promoting them because they are useful, easy to remember, and get results. They are certainly not the only ways to do therapy, but they fit well into a limited time per session framework and really maximize the potential for positive outcome.

Having gone through the opening inquiry, it is now important to make an empathetic statement based on understanding of the patient's experience during the intervening time since the last visit. If there is something positive to focus on, the physician might say, "I would think that you could feel very proud about having handled things in a new way." If the patient has not been successful, a useful intervention could be, "It must be really painful when you are trying so hard to make a change, that things don't seem any different. What do you think you might modify more?"

REPORTING ON HOMEWORK ASSIGNMENTS

After the opening inquiry, focus on the homework assignment: "Do you have the list of options that are available to you?" "Did you talk to your wife and let her know exactly what is troubling you?" "Did you keep a log of all the times that you got very upset?" "What sources of support were you able to come up with?" If the patient has done the assignment, the physician takes this as a positive sign that the patient is exhibiting responsible behavior and is taking control. The session can then focus on what has been learned from the assignment or *one* thing that the patient is most concerned about.

If the assignment has not been done, the physician accepts this fact. It is imperative that the physician not scold or try to induce guilt in the patient. The process of therapy provides new responses to old patterns. The physician communicates to the patient that for some reason the patient chose not to do the assignment at this time, that it might be useful to identify what obstacles were allowed to get in the way of doing the assignment, and that there is always another opportunity.

"Mary, I can understand that you did not take the time to list the activities that really make you feel good. I wonder what makes it so hard for you to focus on things that make you feel good? Do you want to do it for next week, or would you rather talk about it now?" This approach communicates three important messages.

1. It is OK to be where you are. I accept you.
2. You are making choices that have some meaning for you.
3. There may be more constructive choices that you can make.

Starting Where the Patient Is

One of the most important generic principles in doing psychotherapy is that we have to start where the patient is at. This is true in any type of teaching situation. If we are to promote learning of any type, we first have to assess the level of the student's knowledge. If we were to present something that the student already knows, no learning would take place, since the student already has access to that information.[2] If we were to start at a level far more advanced than the student's background preparation, there would also be no learning because the information presented could not be understood or incorporated.

If we are to be effective, we must start where the learner is at this time. We must accept our patients at their current level of functioning and recognize that as we do this without implied criticism, it facilitates their making small but positive changes.

Attentively Listening

Whenever the patient is speaking, the physician should communicate interest and attention. This can be done by maintaining eye contact, leaning toward the patient, and nodding approvingly whenever anything positive is related. It is interesting to note the patient's affect as positive or negative material is being related. Summarizing and reflecting back to the patient what has been heard is useful, since it communicates that the physician has been listening and has understood. It allows the patient to move on.

Probing for Feelings

Probably the most efficient psychotherapeutic strategy is the two-step process of asking patients to identify feelings and then accepting those feelings as appropriate, given the person's subjective experience. When the patient relates what has been happening, good or bad, the physician should inquire, "How did you feel about that?" It is interesting to observe patient's reactions. They often stop, look surprised at the question, think a moment, and then label the feeling. Many people have not had the experience of having an authority figure express interest in their feelings. Often, patients do not respond by labeling a feeling, but instead tell you what they thought or what someone else did. Let us look at an example. Mr. Graham is relating how he asked his wife to make some changes in her schedule to accommodate him and that she agreed without giving him any argument.

> Physician (breaking in): "How did you feel about that?"
> Patient: "I thought she would just refuse to go along with me."
> Physician: "I understand that, but how did it make you *feel*?"
> Patient: "I was surprised and pleased."
> Physician: "You really felt good."

In active listening it is useful to reflect understanding and acceptance by paraphrasing.

A patient has just related that he tried hard to get his wife to listen to how he felt about having to go to her mother's for dinner every Saturday night. Instead of responding, she simply gave him one of her looks and went out of the room.

> Doctor: "So when Ethel walked away, how did you feel? Angry?"
> Patient (nods).
> Doctor: "I can understand that. You must have felt awful."

Giving the patient permission to experience his or her feelings requires minimal investment of time, energy, and understanding. A patient is overheard saying to her friend in the waiting room, "My doctor told me that my feelings are *legitimate*, even if other people see things differently or feel some other way." Her affect would have been appropriate for announcing that she had just won the lottery.

After accepting the patient's feelings, if the physician thinks that it would be useful for the *patient* to become aware of the behavior that contributed to creating the situation, then the next question might be, "Tell me more about that? Then what did you do?" When asking for details or elaboration of events, we encourage focusing on the patient's behavior—what the patient thought and did—not what other people thought and did. The underlying message is that the patient has choices and *the patient has power*. Perhaps the patient was never previously aware of this fact.

Incorporating Medical Treatment

After the opening inquiry is completed, the physician may wish to follow up on any physical complaints. If there is an opportunity to lay on hands, through physical examination, this is useful in helping the patient to connect physical and psychological symptoms. At this time, the physician may also discuss any changes in medications if they are part of the treatment. Medications are always an option to be used along with psychotherapy, as discussed in Chapter 6. However, they should not be seen as part of the ritual offering that the physician presents to the patient, as discussed in Chapter 1. After a brief inquiry into the physical aspects, the physician focuses back on the psychosocial area. "All right, now let's talk about what you are going to do for next week."

Collateral Visits with Family Members

As discussed in Chapter 3, one of the strong advantages the primary physician brings to the therapeutic encounter is the established relationship with the patient and the patient's family. A colleague in solo private practice who trained in our method reports the following case.

> Gail, age 35, moved from Mississippi to New Jersey because of the demands of her husband's job. She is the daughter of alcoholic parents and has been suffering from an anxiety-depression syndrome for years. She has been treated with a variety of tranquilizers and antidepressants and is now struggling to adjust to life in a new community. Because of our inability to find a counselor with whom she felt comfortable, I, as her family physician, agreed to see her for some regular brief sessions. Some of her problems focused on the unresponsiveness of her husband, Jim. She felt that he wouldn't want to come in, but agreed to ask him. I had seen him several times in the office with the children and for problems of his own and was confident I had sufficient rapport to enable us to talk freely.
>
> I began the interview by saying that I understood that it was his wife who had asked for help, but that I felt it was important at this time to elicit his support. During the introductory comments, Jim

assured me that he felt that he had a good relationship with his wife, even though they did not communicate much. It took very little to make him happy. Knowing that his wife and children were provided for and having some peace and quiet for himself were all that he really needed. He realized that his wife needed more, such as a lovely home and an active social life. She also liked to be touched and caressed, but he was not into these things.

"How do you feel about these differences and the obvious lack of communication?" I asked.

He replied that he felt that they should improve their communication and, after some prompting, agreed that it was also probably important to their relationship to pay more attention to each other's interests but he "just hadn't thought much about it."

"For example," I asked, "what do you say when your wife says she wants to redecorate the dining room?"

"I tell her we don't have the money," he replied.

"Is that all?" I asked.

"Yes," he replied, "and the subject is dropped."

"Is there no way you could be more creative about this in order to satisfy your mutual interests?" I queried.

"Like what?" he wanted to know.

"For example, you might get a second job," I said.

"Or she might get a job," he replied quickly. This was something that Gail had been wanting to do, but was afraid her husband would not support. We agreed that this might solve several problems.

Moving on, I asked, "Do you remember your wife on Mother's Day?" (I knew that he had this year.)

"Not usually," he said.

"How about birthdays?"

"Not usually. My family never made much of these things."

"How does she feel when you *do* remember her?" I asked.

"Oh, she loves it."

"Doesn't that give you pleasure also?" I wondered.

"Sure, but I just *don't usually think about it.*"

"And in relation to sex, which you say you like, and touching, which you are not into, are you aware of some common differences between men and women in these areas?"

"Not really."

Here I mentioned some typical needs of women that are often not understood by spouses, which were similar to those expressed by his wife. He seemed quite interested.

As we ended the interview (fifteen minutes, exactly), he brightened up and said that this session had given him new ideas and much to think about, and that he might be glad to talk with me again after he had had time to do some homework.

In this case, the physician, by virtue of her established relationship with the family, in one visit was able to sensitize the husband to some very real problems experienced by his wife, which under normal circumstances he completely excluded from his map. The intervention proved to be extremely effective and Gail's self-esteem increased dramatically as she experienced herself functioning well in her new job and found her husband more attentive to her needs.

FOCUSING THE PATIENT IN THE PRESENT

Since, by definition, we can only act in the here and now, we recommend that the patient generally be focused in the present. The only strong exception to this rule is the person with whom we are working on a grief reaction, who needs to review the history and sort out various feelings about the person, realtionship, object, or position that has been or is about to be lost. This will be discussed in the next chapter.

If a patient complains about how his mother treated him as a child, the physician can respond with some sympathy, but then wonder whether that is really relevant to how the patient presently treats his wife. What is it that the patient can do to get more satisfaction out of his marriage? Also, what is it that the patient wants from his mother now?

Dealing with the Run-on Patient

Often patients will find it difficult to stay within the structure prescribed by the physician. They will elaborate endlessly or they will repeat themselves. It is essential that the physician interrupt and summarize by saying: "Yes, you told me about _____ . I guess that is really important to you. Tell me how it makes you *feel*." They will talk about past events that cannot be changed. Physician: "I hear how upset you are that things didn't work out. How does it make you feel now?"

Getting patients to express guilt, anger, rage, or sadness helps them to accept their feelings and move on. Then they can look at what options there are for dealing with matters now. They will get unstuck and feel less helpless.

Examining Behavioral Options

In general, it is good to focus on options for behavior. In Chapter 7, we introduced the sequence:

1. **What are you feeling?**
2. **What do you want?**
3. **What can you do about it?**

At this point we are helping the patient focus on novel approaches to getting needs met. Encouraging the patient to respond to situations in a different way promotes new behavior. Breaking old destructive patterns is useful even when not at first successful in getting needs met. It demonstrates that there are alternative ways of behaving.

If a wife cannot stop her husband from drinking excessively, she can decide that since there is nothing that she can do to affect his behavior, she can change hers. She will stop arguing and fighting with him, stop aggravating herself about it, and engage instead in some activity that she enjoys. She may also decide to go to Al-Anon and get some support for herself. In this case, the patient has chosen an alternate way of responding to a situation. The situation will not necessarily change, but her perception of it and her response to it will. She feels less overwhelmed.

Exploring Alternate Interpretations of Situations

Another useful approch is to encourage patients to find new ways to interpret situations. Every difficult task can be viewed as an opportunity to gain skill and experience and learn to become stronger or more flexible. The situation can thus become more personally valuable and rewarding than if things had worked out as originally desired or planned.

Patients need to learn that there are *four* options for handling a bad situation.

1. **Leaving it.**
2. **Changing it.**
3. **Accepting it as it is. (And getting support elsewhere.)**
4. **Reframing it. (Interpreting the situation differently.)**

When considering leaving a situation, be it a relationship, job, or other "intolerable" circumstance, patients should be encouraged to assess what the *best* and *worst* possible outcomes might be if they leave. They can then be encouraged to weigh the likelihood of these occurrences. Having a specific strategy to employ will give these patients a sense of competence and power in making the decision. If they decide to leave, they can be encouraged to plan the timing, obtain needed resources and other support, and practice what they want to say when informing various affected parties. This type of behavioral rehearsal fosters a high order of adaptive coping. These behavior rehearsals, or potential scripts, constitute useful homework assignments.

In considering whether a situation can be changed, the patient needs to look at resources that are available and strategies that might be employed. Behavioral change on the part of the patient may ultimately change the responses of significant other people and thereby change the situation. Outside help may be brought to bear on the situation. Sometimes, time alone will cause the situation to change. In this case, it may be appropriate to accept the situation as it is, for the moment.

Accepting a situation as it is and not aggravating oneself thinking about the fact that it should be different is a very constructive option. If a situation is tedious, then interesting and satisfying outside activities can be encouraged. Support groups, close friends, and exercise programs are all means of relieving stress. Taking pride in the quality of one's work and in the interactions with others can also help to make accepting the situation more pleasant.

Changing the interpretation of a situation, that is, reframing or looking at it in a new way, is the most creative and satisfying way of dealing with difficult circumstances. When patients use novel ways of reinterpreting situations they are adapting in a growth-producing fashion, enhancing their mental and physical health.[3] It is the meaning that we attribute to a situation that determines how we feel about it.

> Barbara D. was a patient with multiple problems, including severe back pain that was generally unresponsive to treatment. She was

moderately depressed and very concerned about her demanding husband and her mother-in-law, in whose home they lived. Barbara's treatment included 50 mg of Elavil at bedtime, referral to a biofeedback practitioner, and some assertiveness training. When Barbara complained that her husband "should not be so demanding," the physician suggested that this could be reframed to provide Barbara with the opportunity to practice her assertiveness skills. The change in Barbara's attitude proved remarkable. She simply glowed the following week reporting how she had handled several situations that previously would have left her feeling impotent rage. Not only that, her back pain had almost entirely resolved.

THE PHYSICIAN'S ACCEPTANCE IS PART OF THE TREATMENT

The physician's presence and calm acceptance of the circumstances have beneficial effects on the patient. The physician accepts the patient, the situation, the patients's reaction, but assumes that there are options.

Accepting the patient

The patient feels accepted as a person. The physician's attention is seen as supportive. The patient feels valued, understood, and connected.

Accepting the Situation

By calmly accepting the situation, the physician provides a model for the patient. Together they look at a set of circumstances that, however unfortunate and difficult, need first to be accepted and then handled. Just labeling the situation as a problem changes it.

Accepting the Patient's Reaction

The physician's acceptance of the patient's reaction to the situation is therapeutic. A statement like, "This must be very difficult for you," communicates to the patient that anyone would be stressed in similar circumstances. Usually, it focuses the patient back on his or her strength: "Actually, I'm doing OK, all things considered."

Assuming That There Are Options

Probably the most empowering aspect of the physician's approach is the physician's assumption that there are options. We have talked a great deal in previous chapters about patients' assumptive world view, the map they use to operate in the world. None of us experiences the world directly. We experience subjective representations of circumstances, as we perceive them through our visual, auditory, tactile, or other senses and then interpret this sensory information, based on our previous experience. We filter out cues that do not fit into our previous frame of reference. It is as though there was no such territory on our map. The resulting model of the world that we create determines what choices and limitations we think we have or that we impose on ourselves. when we mistake our limited model of the world for the real world, we limit our options.

When the physician assumes that there are more options than patients are seeing (and it is *not* necessary for the physician to be able to generate them), patients begin to expand their models of the world. They start to include more options and reexamine their limitations. The whole idea of therapy is to help patients be more open to possibilities, look at their world, including themselves, in a new way, and become aware of having choices.

GIVING ADVICE

Physicians are notorious for giving advice. We know that patients ask for advice. They feel dependent, look up to the physician, and often want to be told what to do because they are afraid to make decisions or rely on their own abilities. Because they feel inadequate, they also feel out of control of their own destinies. Giving specific advice is always less effective than focusing patients back on their own resources, with appropriate instructions for developing alternatives. When the physician gives advice, the physician is implying a better understanding of the patient's problems and options than the patient has. This does not empower the patient. Instead, making patients aware of their own abilities and encouraging them to exercise their options is both therapeutic and practical. However, there are certain suggestions that the physican can make. These suggestions focus primarily on the *process* of dealing with problems.

Behavioral Management of Children

When patients are complaining about the behavior of their children, they can be instructed to apply behavioral principles. Primarily, this means reinforcing (rewarding) good behavior and extinguishing (ignoring) inappropriate behavior. Parents are instructed to try to "catch" their children "doing something right"[4] and then reward them. Patients must understand that *attention is a reward*, so parents' acknowledging good behavior consistently instead of focusing attention on bad behavior promotes rapid improvement.

Parents must learn to set strict limits on completely unacceptable or dangerous behavior. They must be instructed to be firm without making threats. Their children must understand that the parents really mean what they say. When a parent says, "If you don't do such and such, I will spank you," that implies that the child has an option. The child has to decide whether doing the forbidden thing is worth the spanking, provided that mother will actually follow through with the threat. If, on the other hand, the clear statment is made, "I don't want you to do that," there is no argument. Patients can be instructed to remove a child from a situation physically, firmly but gently, if necessary, and to institute a *time-out*, a respite in a boring place, as an effective form of discipline.

Parents must be encouraged to allow children to express feelings but not to engage in destructive behavior such as physical violence. When dealing with teenagers, parents should be encouraged to discuss limits with the adolescent involved and to arrive at a joint agreement of acceptable rules. Teenagers must be allowed to take part in the decision-making process and then be held responsible for living up to their commitments. In this way, self-esteem and self-control are taught and the parent stops playing the role of policeman.

Parents must be cautioned not to get into power struggles with the adolescent children. In a power struggle, both parent and child lose, since if the parent wins the battle, the child's sense of power and self-esteem are compromised, generally leading to more destructive behavior. It is more constructive to discuss options jointly and to give the teenager an opportunity to decide between several acceptable alternatives. When parents treat teenagers as though they were responsible individuals, this information becomes part of the children's assumptive world view, and they can be expected to act accordingly.

There are many helpful books that are available to help parents learn the above techniques. Gordon's *Parent Effectiveness Training*[5], and Ginott's *Between Parent and Child*[6] are practical and effective. *Peoplemaking*, by Virginia Satir,[7] is a very readable and useful guide for managing children. All of these are available in paperback. Parents can be encouraged to go to their library and browse. Books can be read and discussed in subsequent sessions. However, it is important that the physican give the usual support: "It must be very difficult to manage a teenager when you have all these other things going on in your life. Let's talk more about that, next time."

Assertiveness Training

Behavioral therapists have found that people can be effectively trained to be more assertive. Patients should be encouraged to ask for what they want. In dealing with other people, patients are encouraged to see themselves and their desires as neither more nor less important than other people or their desires. Patients are encouraged to send "I" messages, learn to state their feelings, ask for what they want, and give their reaction to other people's behavior, for example: "When you ignore me when I walk into the room, I feel discounted," or, "When I make dinner, and you don't come when I call you, I feel very angry." Saying "I don't like it when you don't do what you say you are going to do," is much more effective in getting another person to follow through on a promise than saying, "*You never* do anything you say you are going to do!"

Patients must be encouraged to persevere and repeatedly insist that their rights be respected. Again there are several books that the physician can recommend: Alberti and Emmons's *Your Perfect Right*[8] and Smith's *When I Say No, I Feel Guilty*[9] are two examples. Again, encouragement and permission coming from the physician are more important than the reading of the self-help book. However, the support of the physician along with the outside reading is probably the most effective strategy.

Taking Care of Oneself

One prescription that we encourage the physician to give patients is the instruction to be kind to and take care of themselves. Patients must be told not to make unreasonable demands on themselves when they are under stress. They cannot expect to function at optimal levels and will feel much better if they lower their expectations. They are to give themselves credit for dealing with a difficult situation.

Patients should be encouraged to give themselves treats, take breaks, and plan some desirable activity so that they have something to look forward to. Patients should be encouraged to learn stress management techniques such as focusing on breathing, progressive relaxation, or meditation. They need to be encouraged to exercise regularly, choosing a modality they enjoy, and also need to learn to monitor and change their thinking patterns.

Distinguishing Between Thoughts, Feelings, and Behavior

It is highly useful to make patients aware of the distinctions between thoughts, feelings, and behavior. Thoughts are constant internal messages that are often not noticed, but are powerful enough to create our most intense emotions. We are constantly describing the world to ourselves and judging whether things are the way we want them to be. Based on these judgments, we decide whether things are good or bad, painful, dangerous, or just not as they should be.[10,11] Our thoughts then influence the way that we feel about a situation. Feelings are an automatic emotional response based on our interpretation of an event. Feelings must be accepted.

Given our interpretation of a situation (based on our map of the world), we feel as we do. However, therapy may consist of challenging the underlying value judgments and assumptions that determine what we think. If we modify what we think and change our judgments, our feelings will change.

Behavior is a voluntary action. We choose our behavior. If we are in touch with our feelings, we can learn to control our behavior. Our behavior is probably the only thing in life we really can control, and should be aimed at getting us what we want and presenting ourselves to the world as we wish to be seen. A physician can be very angry with a patient but not let this show by choosing words carefully, in order not to intimidate the patient and maximize the patient's cooperation.

Taking Responsibility for Our Feelings

The last specific advice we suggest that physicians offer patients is that it is useful to take responsibility for our own feelings. Few people realize that no one can actually make us feel anything. We feel the way we do as an automatic response to our interpretation of our situation. A change in interpretation changes the feeling. For example, if we feel that *all* physicians reading this book should agree with our approach to therapy, we will feel very badly if some reviewers object to parts of this book or don't like it. On the other hand, if we hope that a few people will find this book helpful and use the techniques that we are proposing, we will be delighted if some people let us know that they are finding it useful.

Our current level of self-esteem, expectation for the future, and general outlook determines how we feel more than what actually happens to us. It is the physician's task to make the patient aware that we make ourselves feel hurt, angry, frustrated, and rejected by the way that we talk to ourselves about what has happened or is going to happen. These feelings are bad and painful. If we are going to turn off the pain, we must first become aware of what we are feeling, then learn to modify those feelings through reinterpretation of our circumstances.

ENDING THE SESSION

Ending the session on time is important for both physician and patient. It is an affirmation of the patient's ability to cope and apply the one or two strategies discussed in the session, and it insures that the contract is valid and that the physician intends to follow through. It secures the sense of connection.

At the end of the allotted time, the physician should make an honest comment focusing on some positive aspect of how the patient is dealing with the situation. The physician may express the feeling that it would be nice if there were more time (it lets the patient know that the physician values the contact) but that the discussion will be continued at the next scheduled session. The importance here is keeping the connection. The patient is instructed to call if something serious changes in the meantime.

HOMEWORK

The specific homework task is jointly determined for the intervening time. The patient makes a contract with the physician agreeing to keep a journal, order the priority of problems, find a specific book, and/or in general monitor changes in behavior and the resultant consequences.

It is important that the time spent with the physician be devoted to building skills that the patient can use to change interactions with the significant others in the patient's life. The visit with the physician provides direction and helps make the patient aware of options and the personal power to put them into effect. All of this is part of the homework that will be examined at the next session. Knowing that the physician will be expecting a report helps motivate the patient to follow through on the assignment.

> Carol G., a 22-year-old white female and mother of two children, ages three and five, currently living with a boy friend, came to the office complaining of two weeks of dizziness. She seemed totally overwhelmed by the multiple problems in her life. For a homework assignment, the physician suggested that Carol keep a diary and record all instances of dizziness and the particular circumstances when they occurred. On returning the following week, Carol was able to recognize that her dizziness occurred primarily when she felt most out of control in dealing with her estranged husband, her in-laws, her child's teacher, and her mother. For the following week she was given the assignment to do one thing nice for herself. The resulting change was dramatic. Carol had decided to have lunch with a friend—leaving her mother to babysit—talked through her problems, and finally contacted a lawyer to start divorce proceedings.

ALLOCATING TIME

In general, the patient should be allowed to talk about twelve minutes out of the fifteen. Brief comments from the physician should keep the patient focused on one or two tasks that can be used as preparation for the next session. By only dealing with one or two issues during a particular session, the patient does not become confused or overloaded. The physician is teaching a process and treating a person.

In the next chapter, we will look at some specific approaches to difficult situations. We will give some suggestions for treating the hypochondriacal patient, the grieving patient, the depressed patient, the suicidal patient and the patient that must be referred because the physician feels uncomfortable.

Now let us look at a case that was handled by a young physician under our supervision and is typical of the effective outcome that can be expected over time.

> Daniel G., a 16-year-old white male, presented at the family practice center on Tuesday afternoon in late November complaining of dizzy spells. The previous Sunday he had felt light-headed, dizzy, and actually passed out. The patient said there had been two or three previous episodes but denied recent fever, palpitations, or chest pain.
>
> The patient and his mother had recently moved into the area to live with the patient's grandmother. The patient related that he had no friends and was mostly interested in his baseball card collection. He admitted that he felt badly about the fact that he had no father and that his mother was crippled and confined to a wheelchair. The patient revealed that he wanted to become a carpenter.
>
> A physical examination including a complete neurological exam was normal, allowing the physician to rule out for the moment an impending catastrophic medical event. His impression was vasovagal syncopal episodes. For completeness, routine labs were ordered, but the physician was more concerned that this patient needed emotional support. The patient was a shy, sensitive individual with many emotional problems and no one to talk to. This made him feel very depressed. The physician made a contract for follow-up in one week with the expressed intention of seeing the patient for counseling.
>
> In the course of having blood drawn the patient became dizzy, his blood pressure dropped to 60/40, reinforcing the contention that this patient's symptoms were manifestations of vagal activity. In a half hour it returned to normal and the patient was released.
>
> The patient returned the following week. There had been no further episodes of dizziness. The patient started to talk about his home situation. There was a horrendous history of abuse on the part of a man living with the mother and constant moves. The physican gave support and focused the patient on the present situation. Dan had made a new friend in school and felt good about that, but he expressed a desire to transfer to vocational school The physician said he would look into that.
>
> A contract was made to see the patient regularly once a week for fifteen minute sessions. The third week, Dan appeared nervous

and depressed. His affect was rather flat. He seemed to have nothing much to say. He wondered why the physician was interested in seeing him. The physician said that he enjoyed talking with Dan and would help him to learn to make other friends and focus on planning his life.

By the fourth week the patient was much more cooperative. He was happy about a project in school and spontaneously started to share some of his interests. Christmas week the patient canceled his appointment. He arrived early in January complaining of a head cold but feeling much happier. It was during this session that the patient revealed a history of sexual abuse several years previously and expressed how happy he was to be receiving counseling. The physician assured Dan that is was not his fault that he had been abused and that it must have been awful for him. This seemed to relieve the boy. The subject was brought up several weeks later, but seemed to have lost its impact.

Dan was seen regularly for counseling every other week. Over time, he became involved with the golf club at school and made one close friend. He was treated for a sore throat, some nose bleeds, and developed a very relaxed and trusting relationship with his doctor. After about a year, his afternoon job prevented him from attending his sessions regularly. A sports physical clearing him for team participation is the last item in the chart. When Dan moved away a year and a half later, he seemed to be a rather confident, reasonably well-adjusted young man who was clear on his goals and directed toward achieving them.

SUMMARY

When starting a therapy session, the opening inquiry should focus on the present situation, a report on the homework assignment, and the best and worst things that happened since the previous visit. The physician always starts where the patient is at and communicates interest through attentive listening. Questions should generally probe for feelings and what the patient personally did in response to circumstances. Medication and laying on of hands through examinations and collateral visits with family members constitute options that can be incorporated.

In general, the patient should be focused in the present. Options available for handling painful situations include leaving it, changing it, accepting it with additional support, and reframing or reinterpreting it.

Physicians must gently set limits on the amount of detail or repetition that a patient presents. The physican should be supportive of the patient. The physician's acceptance is therapeutic. He or she accepts the patient, the situation, and the patient's reaction to the situation, but assumes that there are options.

In giving advice, the physician focuses on the process of dealing with problems rather than their content. Advice may be given regarding behavioral strategies for managing children, becoming assertive, and taking care of oneself. The physcan points out the difference between thoughts, feelings, and behavior and how thoughts (judgments) may be modified with resulting emotional changes. Patients are held responsible for their own feelings. At the end of the session, the physician extends the contract through the assignment of homework and the expectation that the patient will return to report on a particular task that was accomplished. During the session the patient should speak about thirteen minutes with brief comments from the physician that focus on constructive elements.

REFERENCES

1. Antonovsky, A. *Health, Stress, and Coping.* San Francisco: Jossey-Bass, 1979.
2. Whitman, N. A. and Schwenk, T. L. *Preceptors as Teachers: A Guide to Clinical Teaching.* Salt Lake City, UT: University of Utah School of Medicine Press, 1984.
3. Vaillant, G. E.. Natural history of male psychologic health: Effects of mental health on physical health. *New England Journal of Medicine*, 1979, 301, 1249-1254.
4. Blanchard, K. and Johnson, S. *The One Minute Manager.* New York: Morrow, 1982.
5. Gordon, T. *Parent Effectiveness Training.* New York: Wyden, 1970.
6. Ginott, H. G. *Between Parent and Child.* New York: Avon Books, 1969.
7. Satir, V. *Peoplemaking.* Palo Alto, CA: Science and Behavior Books, 1972.
8. Alberti, R. E. and Emmons, M. *Your Perfect Right*, rev. ed. San Luis Obispo, CA: Impact Press, 1974.
9. Smith, M. J. *When I Say No, I Feel Guilty.* New York: Dial Press, 1975.
10. Beck, A. T. *Cognitive Therapy and Emotional Disorders.* New York: New American Library, 1979.
11. Ellis, A. *A New Guide to Rational Living.* North Hollywood, CA: Wilshire Books, 1975.

9
Handling Special Patients and Situations

In this chapter we would like to address a potpourri of issues that have not been discussed in sufficient detail up to now. There are patients that are hard to treat because they are hard to be with. How can we relate to them? There are suicidal patients who pose a danger to themselves, addicted patients, hostile patients, and depressed patients, to mention only a few. Can we help them? And most important, can we help them without feeling totally put upon, without feeling burned out, so that we are not able to relate with sufficient empathy to other patients? There are also problems related to dealing with family members, especially when they present a divided or self-righteous front. Is there a way to handle these situations smoothly? We think so.

We also want to talk about constructive approaches that can be taught to nurses, receptionists, and other staff members that will cut down on some patients' frustration and anxiety, thereby facilitating their receptivity to physician input. Finally, we would like to address the application of psychotherapeutic (cognitive) principles for the personal benefit of the physician. In other words, since this is a book on applied psychotherapy, we will actualize the principle, "Physician heal thyself."[1]

DEALING WITH DIFFICULT PATIENTS

Groves[2] wrote an article, provocatively entitled "Taking Care of the Hateful Patient," in which he developed four stereotypes of particularly difficult patient personalities and behavioral categories. Groves divided hateful patients into dependent clingers, manipulative help-rejectors, entitled demanders, and self-destructive deniers. Physicians are sorely tried by contact with these types of patients. These individuals precipitate negative feelings on the part of physicians who feel depleted by the need to provide endless emotional supplies, when no objective positive outcome seems to result. After describing symptom differences and similarities, Groves develops specific approaches for dealing with each of these patient types. Our approach is simpler. We start by believing that each patient is behaving in the best possible way, for this patient, at this time. That does not mean that it will always be that way, but it is that way now. People make fundamental changes when properly motivated either in response to catastrophe or by a series of small steps. We vote for the small steps.

Except in situations posing an immediate threat to life or limb, we suggest that physicians limit contact with patients that arouse negative emotions to no more than fifteen minutes, regardless of the complexity of the problems or lists of complaints. During that time the physician is encouraged to integrate medical and psychosocial concerns, treating the patient in the context of the total life situation. If there are too many problems for one visit, the patient can be brought back the following week. This has the additional payoff of demonstrating the physician's interest. It addresses the patient's needs in a supportive manner. The patient will feel *less* rejected (and these patients are highly skilled at getting doctors and others to reject them) in having frequent brief sessions. Ultimately this will result in much better utilization of time, since there will not be lengthy and frustrating sessions of miscommunication. It has been our experience that patients learn to organize the details of their stories to fit into the time available. The physician may have to take charge quite directly by saying something like, "I can hear that you have several things that really bother you, and that there is very little cooperation at home, but I need to understand what, specifically, you would like me to do for you today."

One of the techniques that we can apply is to learn to reframe the situations that give us the most problems and to look at them as providing us with the opportunity to practice the skills that we have been promoting in this book. So rather than thinking, "Oh, good grief, it's Mrs. Brown. I hate to see her since she has numerous problems, doesn't take her medicine, never feels grateful, never gets better, or stops complaining," we can think, "Oh, it's Mrs. Brown. I feel sorry that she is so needy. I have an opportunity to try out some of these new techniques. I will let her talk about two minutes. I will try to respond with something positive. Then, after I find out what is going on in her life, I will ask her to concentrate on one specific problem and try to get to identify one small change that she can make to make herself feel better. If I can make the time with her more productive, I will feel good. I will aim for one small win, and limit the time with her to no more than fifteen minutes."

If the physician learns to reframe the situation and take satisfaction from dealing with difficult patients in a smooth and effective manner, the practice of medicine may well become more gratifying. Seeing people relax, become less anxious, hostile, or demanding is a tremendous experience. As we change our approach, unreasonable patients may actually become more reasonable.

Patients are sometimes unpleasant, critical, and hostile. Many times patients are frustrated, tired of not feeling or functioning well, and tired of being dependent on doctors who are not always able to help them; therefore, they become hostile. They are so sure that they will not get their needs met that their attitude and behavior guarantees completion of the self-fulfilling prophecy. We are suggesting that there is a way to break this pattern. By acknowledging the patient's frustration instead of demanding that it be held in check, the situation is immediately changed. Let us look at some practical examples.

The Hypochondriacal Patient

Perhaps the most difficult patients to deal with over time are the hypochondriacal patients, whose preoccupation with real or imagined illnesses tries the patience of the most dedicated physician.[3,4] These patients focus the greatest part of their time and attention on their physical symptoms and seem determined to suffer loudly while being unsuccessful in finding anyone to cure them. These patients need to be scheduled for regular visits at predetermined intervals (every two weeks for starters is often tolerable for both patient and physician) whether or not they are complaining about acute symptoms.

Letting these patients know that they will get regular care whether or not they are feeling acutely bad is the first positive step in managing the hypochondriasis. After acknowledging their concerns about their current symptoms and emphasizing that it must be awful not to ever feel well, it is essential to follow the BATHE protocol during every visit. It is also very important to record important psychosocial data so that inquiries can be made about outcomes of situations in the patient's life. This communicates that the physician is interested in the patient as a whole person and not just in the patient as a collection of disease symptoms. The patient does not have to be sick to get attention or a response.

As we have said, it is important to acknowledge patients' physical suffering and allow them a reasonable amount ot time to discuss it, but always to put things back into the context of the patient's life: "How does that affect your ability to spend time with your grandchildren?" "What can you do to maximize enjoyment of the times when you feel good?"

Over time, this approach may offer these patients the opportunity to focus on other aspect of life besides physical complaints. Their previous life experience may have led these patients to believe that care and attention could only be gotten through illness-related behavior. Now there are alternatives. By structuring therapy regularly and including broader aspects of the patient's experience, the physican can treat the hypochondriac quite successfully. We again caution physicians not to let the length of the session exceed their own tolerance for contact with this type of patient. Perhaps it will be necessary to limit the time to seven or eight minutes. The session would start with the physician making this clear: "Mary, we have about eight minutes. Tell me what you are most concerned about this week?" Since there are regularly scheduled visits, each session can focus on one or two problems. Our experience has been that patients respond very well to this type of treatment. After a while, they will tolerate longer periods between visits, but will usually need to be seen at least once every six weeks, or they will regress. It is also important to allow these patients to keep at least one or two symptoms. Watzlawick[5] has pointed out how critical it is to always allow patients the unresolved remnant.

The Chronic Complainer

There is a subtle difference between hypochondriacs who are truly anxious regarding the state of their health (sometimes referred to as the worried well) and the chronic complainers[6] representing a group of troublesome patients who have multiple complaints, feel the need to be seen frequently, and fit into the group of entitled demanders so aptly described by Groves.[2] These patients rarely get well and never seem to appreciate the efforts the physician makes on their behalf. It would appear obvious that these patients need their disease in order to function at all.

> Mary S. has been seeing Dr. L. for almost eight months on a regular basis. She is a 47-year-old, divorced, obese, white female with moderately well-controlled hypertension who also complains of insomnia and a variety of aches and pains. Mary had been laid off from her job as a factory worker and been put on temporary disability payments. She is very angry because her benefits are about to expire, she has problems paying her rent, argues constantly with her 21-year-old son who lives with her, and feels that her married daughter and son-in-law treat her badly. Mary talks loudly and quickly. It is as though she wants to get twenty minutes of conversation into a ten minute session. Dr. L. usually feels as though he has been assaulted or perhaps run over by a lawn mower after spending any amount of time with her. Routine lab work and careful examination have convinced Dr. L. that Mary's problems are primarily stress induced, stress that she generates for herself and others. He has developed a clinical style that allows his patient the first minutes of the interview to complain about whatever is bothering her the most, after which he takes control and examines one problem in detail. After monitoring medications and laying on hands, Dr. L. wonders what Mary could do differently in a specific interaction with her son. He sees her regularly, every two weeks. Her improvement becomes obvious, and she grows aware that she has power to make things happen, and not just by being demanding. There are even indications that, since she feels accepted, she is learning to listen (a little).

There is a growing body of contemporary literature focusing on various somatization disorders.[7-14] The basics of psychosomatic medicine were proposed in the 1943 article by Franz Alexander,[15] in which he explained that some patients experiencing certain emotions, such as anger, fear, frustration, neediness, or sorrow do not express them because of internal conflict and develop the physical symptoms that were concomitants of the emotion. Psychiatrists will contend that once these emotions can be expressed directly, the need to somatize will be decreased.[16]

In contrast, the stress-response (and the stress can be self-induced, as it is with the chronic complainer) emotions are acutely felt and trigger physiological reactions that then become chronic and actually precipitate organic problems. Patients experience the physiological symptoms that are the result of sympathetic arousal that does not get discharged productively. Many patients do not know how to get any kind of care or attention without complaining. When their complaints are not effective, they persevere and complain louder and longer. This increases stress.

The effectiveness of cognitive interventions that help people to reinterpret situations, thereby changing the actual emotional reaction, becomes obvious. Until patients become aware of the mechanisms involved and their power to ameliorate their reations, they are trapped. Anyone who is trapped or pushed into a corner is not very nice to deal with. Anything that the physician can do to empower patients and slowly, over time, convince them that they can affect their health, the course of their lives, and get their needs met through more direct strategies than by complaining about physical symptoms is highly therapeutic.

When the chronic complainer bemoans the fact that his wife offers him no sympathy, the physician can respond; "I can see that that is very difficult for you. What is it, specifically, that you want from your wife?"

Patient: "I want her to pay attention to me."

Doctor: "That makes sense. Does she pay attention when you tell her about your pain?"

Patient: "No, she ignores me. Then she starts complaining about her headaches."

Doctor: "I see. Is there anything that you can do to change the situation?"

If the patient responds negatively, it is important not to argue. Power struggles are not constructive. When we convince patients that they are wrong, we lose, because we damage these patients' self-esteem. In Chapter 3, we pointed out the enormous power that is attributed to physicians and how that power can be used therapeutically to great advantage. It can also be used detrimentally, to diminish the patient.

Is is useful to try to get the patient to commit to doing one small task that has a positive and realistic potential. When the patient says that his wife complains about her headaches, perhaps the patient could give *her* the kind of sympathetic response he desires. It would certainly get her *attention*.

It is crucial to be aware that one of the great differences between inpatient and outpatient medicine is that in the outpatient setting the physician has no control over what the patient actually does. In that connection it is important to find a way to get the patient to want to do what is necessary. The patient must agree willingly, or the patient will sabotage the physician's best efforts. The patient must be convinced that there is a payoff for trying. Tasks must be feasible and then small wins will accumulate and make big differences.

The Substance Abuser

It is no accident that the literature on physician referrals to psychiatrists shows the highest rate of referrals for patients with various substance abuse or addictive disorders.[17,18] Alcohol or narcotics abusers are difficult to treat because, by definition, these patients do not exercise control or take responsibility for their behavior.

If a physician wishes to get involved with this type of patient, then the appropriate model may be the enlightened model[19] (see Chapter 4) in which the assumption is made that the patient *is* responsible for having created the situation—because the patient is trying to run away from rather than dealing with problems, and because the patient cannot take responsibility for solving the situation alone and must agree to follow the instruction of the physician who will attempt to help. A firm contract must be made with the patient committing to abstinence from the drug of choice (or other nonprescribed chemicals), following the physician's orders explicitly, and most of all reporting any infringement of these conditions. Firm limits must be set, and the contract depends on the patient's compliance.

The Depressed Patient

It can be very depressing to have to spend time with depressed patients. There is something contagious in the negativity, heaviness, hopelessness, and neediness expressed by these unhappy people. It is important to set realistic expectations for the patient and ourselves. The patient can be expected to suffer, but can be encouraged to make some small changes, minute ones, if necessary. Klein and Seligman[20] have demonstrated conclusively that getting people to do small tasks at which they succeed can reverse the learned helplessness, which is the correlate of depression. So, in treating a depressed patient, we first give the patient permission to be depressed. We do *not* suggest that the patient should feel any different than he or she does. We do not focus the patient on the positive features of his or her life. That only sets up resistance in the patient. We also encourage the family to stop trying to cheer the patient up. Patients who are depressed and are told to look on the bright side of things or to count their blessings, often feel misunderstood, wrong, ungrateful, or a variety of other unpleasant feelings that simply exacerbate their underlying depression. Instead, we agree that it seems as though *right now* things are really bad and we can understand that the patient would feel awful. Sometimes, if we are lucky, the patient will actually respond with something positive. Perversity is an endemic human quality.

Treatment consists of challenging some of the assumptions and generalities that the patient makes and suggesting one activity that will give the patient a subjective sense of control: "Start to walk, perhaps ten minutes a day." "Do one nice thing for yourself each day." "Make a written list of all the tasks you have to do, and feel that you can't. Then do just one. The one that takes the least time."

The physician must not expect to change the patient's situation, but can be expected to see the patient regularly, be supportive (lead to the patient's strength), prescribe and monitor medications (if appropriate), and set reasonable limits on the patient's allowable wallowing time. Labeling wallowing for what it is and setting a five minute limit on this activity at any given time is very effective.

The Grieving Patient

In Chapter 6 we pointed out that therapy for grief can usually be accomplished in six to eight sessions. Whenever a patient appears to be overreacting to a current loss, an unresolved grief reaction may well be contributing to the severity of the response. The physician needs to probe in order to ascertain if this is true. The physician then explains the significance of completing the mourning process and how difficult this sometimes is because of the ambivalence that most of us feel toward the significant others in our lives and the discomfort with the anger that is generated when we are abandoned through death or other circumstances. It is important for the patient to talk about these feelings as well as reviewing the significant aspects of the lost relationship. The six or eight sessions do not necessarily have to occur weekly. In a resistant patient, the physician can simply bring up the subject briefly every time that the patient is seen for any medical problem. However, ideally, the patient will be cooperative and willing to work. Because therapy for grief requires a thorough airing of the issues, reminiscing about important details, homework in the form of writing about the person, talking to relatives or friends, and reviewing snapshots are crucial. The fifteen minute session with the physician can then be used to highlight important understandings.

Anniversary reactions[21] are extremely common and patients benefit from being told to expect a variety of somatic symptoms and mood shifts around the anniversary date of a loss or other significant event. Patients primarily need to be given encouragement to feel their pain, rather than try to shut it off. There is little that is required of the physician except to be there.

The Suicidal Patient

When working with depressed or grieving patients, suicide is always a potential risk. These patients are experiencing such a high degree of subjective pain that the need to turn off the pain may make the option of killing themselves appear to be quite attractive. In general, serious consideration of suicide corresponds with serious feelings of poor self-esteem, lack of social support, and lack of hope. People who talk about suicide *will* do it, if their attempts to get help fail.

We have suggested that the primary care physican can treat potentially suicidal patients very effectively. Once these patients feel that someone is really concerned about them, they must readjust their notion that there is no one in the world who cares and that *everyone* would be better off if they were dead. The physician acknowledges that suicide is a potential option that may seem desirable at a given time, *but* once exercised, it excludes all other options. It really is permanent. Since it is *always* better to keep one's options open, the physician might say, "I hate to see you use a permanent solution for what may turn out to be a temporary problem. Why don't we see how you feel in a few weeks. Let's take it one day at a time and see if, together, we can't find a better way to deal with this situation."

However, in dealing with the suicidal patient, the doctor must be available for the patient when the patient needs to feel connected. If the doctor is going to be away and someone else will be on call, the covering physician must be informed about the seriousness of the situation and the support that must be given. It is hoped that family and friends will also be mobilized. One of the tasks given the patient is to ask for support from significant others. The patient must be given clear instructions to call at a specific time when the physician will be personally available to talk. It is important to have the patient verify the commitment to call at such and such a time, or to come in for an appointment in two days, or whatever time period is mutually agreeable. Once patients clearly promise to call or come in at a specific time in the future, they are making a statement that they expect to be around at that time. A *note* to that effect must be put into the chart: "Patient promises to call tomorrow to check in. Will be seen on Wednesday for follow-up. Patient instructed to go to ER if situation worsens."

Handling Difficult Family Members

Dealing with the patient's family can be one of the most rewarding or frustrating aspects of practicing medicine. Often family members will call and provide unsolicited information about a patient or make suggestions about treatment. Most physicians are clear on the implications of confidentiality issues and will not share information about the patient, but may feel stressed by the lack of clarity regarding the relationship with the family member. In this connection, we would suggest that physicians not get into a power struggle and in general avoid confrontations. We always assume that family members have their own agenda, but we are not responsible for figuring out what their issues are or making judgments as to their merit.

Avoiding power struggles or offending family members are important considerations. We suggest that the physician learn to practice a form of verbal aikido. Aikido is a Japanese martial art that is sometimes referred to as "the dance." When a person who is skilled in aikido is attacked, the automatic response is to turn quickly, join with the attacker, and go along in the direction of the attack. Then after a few seconds, the practitioner gently turns both himself and the attacker around, so that they are both going in the other direction. After this, he or she can gracefully disengage or knock the attacker out.

Verbally, this translates into always giving acknowledgment of the legitimacy of others' requests or positions. It catches them off guard and leaves them open to hearing what the physician has to say. By first showing respect for the family member's position and anxiety, the physician defuses any potential defensiveness. So when making treatment or discharge plans or discussing anything with a family member, we suggest that the physician automatically start with the phrase: "I can hear how concerned you are, but. . . [then state your case]." If it is more comfortable, you may prefer to say, "I know you care a great deal about your mother, (father), (husband), (son), (aunt), (niece), (etc.), but. . . ."

It is irrelevant whether you actually subscribe to the above statement. Making the statement is a simple strategy that gets you the other person's attention and positive receptivity. The same thing can be accomplished by starting with the phrase, "I agree with you that. . . [and find some part of their suggestion that you can accept]."

People hear better if someone starts by agreeing with them. The critical issue here is that the more difficult and demanding family members are—regardless of whether you see any merit in their suggestions or even feel that they have a legitimate stake in the outcome—there is nothing to be gained by direct antagonism. Hence the effectiveness of this technique.

You may say to yourself, "That drunken bum hasn't given two hoots about his mother in the last five years. Why should he tell me how to treat her?"

You may be *absolutely right*, but it will be more difficult to deal with him if you confront him with that now. Instead we say, "I can see how concerned you are. This must be very difficult for you. I am really glad you are letting me know what you would like me to do, *but* my impression, [clinical judgment, good medical practice] demands that I do such and such. I will keep you informed." In a later section, we will discuss the technique for direct confrontation, when it becomes absolutely necessary.

Another important consideration to keep in mind when dealing with families is that often there are large elements of guilt. When the son from Chicago suddenly calls you and demands that absolutely everything be done for his father, whom he has neglected for years, it is a clear sign that an attempt is being made to resolve guilt. We suggest that physicians absolve family members of guilt whenever possible. Very often guilt is projected resentment. But, in any case, guilt is such an unpleasant emotion that concomitant hostility is generated toward the person who makes us feel guilty. Actually, guilt and hostility are opposite sides of the same coin. It is always therapeutic to say, "I know that you did as much as you could." That's always true. It may not have been enough for the other person, but if they could have done more (given their map), they would have. Do *not* say, "You have no reason to feel guilty." Just say, "I'm sure that you've expressed your love, as best you could. No one can expect more than that."

All of these interventions are designed to facilitate communications but allow us to practice according to our best judgment. It is like aikido in that instead of meeting the opponent head-on and absorbing the impact of his or her forward movement, we come from the side, join in the other's movement, and then effectively spin our opponent around. It's fun. Reframing also helps. Instead of thinking, "Why do I have to deal with all of these impossible people?" (and it is clear that some people are more impossible than others) we think, "Here is an opportunity to practice my new skills and see how I make out." To the upset husband we say, "I know you have Jane's interest at heart, *but* at this time I must do what she wants. In the long run, it will be very beneficial for her, which I know is what you want."

Dealing with Conflict Between Family Members

In dealing with family members who disagree over goals and strategies, it is most important to acknowledge the legitimacy of each person's position and reaction. Remember, they all have different maps. They all experience their family in a unique way. In trying to achieve some sort of consensus, it is important they they focus on a superordinate goal—the welfare of the patient. It they cannot agree, then perhaps the physician's best judgment of the patient's needs will have to prevail. If the physician has been supportive of the family and the patient, it is likely that they will agree on this. The physician takes responsibility because the physician has control of the treatment (moral model). Working with the family is an important challenge and lends itself to creative interventions by the physician that are beyond the scope of this book.[22]

Confronting the Patient

There are times when a person's behavior goes beyond acceptable limits or causes a problem, making confrontation necessary. Under these circumstances, it is important to point out to the person how the behavior is a problem, that is, how it affects the physician, the staff, or the practice, and to suggest a specific correction. Sometimes this is enough, and the person apologizes and makes the correction. More often, the person becomes defensive, abusive, and will not discuss the issue. The way that people react to being confronted with something negative about themselves that they do not wish to acknowledge (it's on their map, but they pretend it isn't) or do not wish to change is usually stereotypical.[23] People will react as though they had been *zapped*. We can expect one of three potential behaviors in response to a *zap*: counterattack, retreat, or diffusion.

Counterattack: "Really doctor, I have not been pleased with the way that you treated my mother. I think I will ask someone else to take over her care."

Retreat: "I'm sorry, doctor, I don't have time to discuss it now (or ever). I'm late for an appointment."

Diffusion: "You think that I'm hard to deal with. My son has been giving me so much trouble lately. What do you think is wrong with the current generation?"

Any of these reactions are typical for persons being zapped, having to deal with something they do not want to have to deal with. It is important not to get caught in feeling counterzapped but to switch to active listening and verbal aikido and then repeat your message. If you expect the negative reaction, you are prepared to handle it smoothly: "Yes, I agree that sometimes you have not been pleased with the treatment choices, *but* you must cease bringing alcohol into the hospital." "Mr. Jones. I know you are in a hurry, *but* I want you to get that blood test done today." "Yes, I can see how frustrated you are with your son, but I must have your signed consent for this prodecure, now." "Mrs. Smith, I understand how angry you are when I sometimes don't call you right back, how your boss makes unreasonable demands on you at work, and how unreliable your babysitter is, *but* I cannot continue to treat your diabetes if you will not take your medicine as prescribed."

Anytime we confront another with something they really don't want to hear from us, it can be considered a zap. Zaps by definition are subjective experiences of the receiver, who will react (or rather overreact) in typical fashion. Recognizing this as normal, being prepared for it, and not reacting to the counterattack of the *zappee* as though it were a *zap* are very useful. Retreats or diversions can also be expected and must at first be accepted before reiteration of the initial problem can be productive. Sometimes, it is necessary to go through several rounds before finally being heard. This insight is helpful in all interpersonal situations involving conflict that must be addressed.

TRAINING THE OFFICE STAFF

The office staff represents an important element of the environment that the patient experiences when coming to the physician for treatment. In fact, when calling to make an appointment or wanting to speak to the physician on the phone, the staff acts as the ultimate gatekeeper.

It is important that receptionists and nursing personnel become aware of the effects of stress on patients as outlined in Chapter 2 and learn a few simple and effective interventions for managing their interactions with patients. Our receptionist complained that some patients are very difficult and demanding on the phone and that *they* should learn to be more cooperative. Patients who are upset are often unreasonable. It is not useful to focus on the fact that they should not be that way; the reality is that they are. The question becomes: "What can be done to make the person feel supported enough so that healthier responses can be expected? How can we deal with these people without contributing to our own stress?"

Fielding Phone Calls

Sometimes when a physician has not returned a patient's call, for whatever reason, the patient will become frustrated and abusive of the staff. We certainly do not condone this type of behavior, but it is not useful for the receptionist to get upset and respond angrily to the patient. What is helpful is for the receptionist to make a supportive statement: "It must be difficult to have to stay home and wait for the doctor to call back, when you have so much to do." "It must be hard when you are worried about Nancy's fever to not be able to reach the doctor right away. Time passes so slowly when you're anxious, doesn't it?" This type of understanding response makes the patient feel supported and connected to another human being who acknowledges the reaction to the stress as being reasonable—which it is!

The second major factor that the staff must be encouraged to do is to help the patient set realistic expectations. It is of little value to get the patient off the phone by saying, "Yes, I'll tell the doctor to call you right away," when the doctor is not back from lunch, solidly booked with patients all afternoon, and has to make hospital rounds after 5 before going to an out-of-town medical society dinner at 7:30 P.M. Instead, it is better to say that the doctor will probably not be available to speak to the patient and ask if there is a specific question that needs to be answered or "can it wait till morning?"

It is important to specify when to expect the doctor's call. The implication is that the patient's time is also valuable and that the patient has other things to do besides just wait for the physician to phone back. If it becomes impossible for the physician to contact the patient within the agreed time period, someone else should call and inform the patient *when* the physician can be expected to be free.

We like to compare the experience of the patient to ours, when we are phoning someone whose line is busy and we are put on hold. It is very reassuring to have the operator periodically break in and report that the line is still busy. The wait is no less interminable, but we know that we have not been forgotten. There is a sense of being acknowledged and still being connected. We need to be sure that patients do not feel forgotten and disconnected. If these procedures are adopted, there will be a minimum of angry repeat calls from frustrated patients.

Patients in the Office

There are also potential problems connected with patients in the office. Because of their particular personalities, certain patients are extremely difficult for the staff to deal with. We know that the patients' personalities are not going to change, but often their behavior can be managed more effectively. Objectively, these patients' problems may not be serious; subjectively, their problems are disturbing their precarious equilibrium or they would not be coming to the doctor for help. The staff needs to understand that patients under stress will not be at their best behavior. They may become demanding, unreasonable, angry, unhappy, and impatient with the staff, though often passive or ingratiating with the physician on whom they feel dependent.

The staff needs to learn to set reasonable limits, always acknowledging patients' rights to feel as they do, but asserting the need to control their behavior. Letting patients who are reciting a laundry list of troubles, insults, and concerns know that, "I understand how difficult it must be for you," or "I can see how upset you are," or, "I can hear how angry and frustrated you feel, *but* . . ." saves patients from continued efforts to convince someone of their plight. Once they have successfully communicated that they are unhappy, they will be more apt to be able to hear what others want.

The staff also needs to help the patient set realistic expectations for the visit. It is better to say that there will be at least a half hour wait when the doctor is running behind schedule than to say nothing or worse yet, "The doctor will be right with you," when the doctor will not be right with them. When patients feel as though their comfort is a concern for others, it is more likely that they will be able to respond to the concerns of other people.

Care for the Caring

The physician has a responsibility to support the staff while encouraging concern for patient well-being. We would remind the physician that the staff needs to feel competent and connected also. It is important that the physician frequently acknowledge the contribution that the staff is making to the supportive environment of the office: "I really appreciate the way you've handled Mrs. Brown. She must be very difficult for you to deal with." "You must really get tired of having to field all these phone calls when I sometimes have trouble getting back to these people."

RULES FOR PHYSICIAN SURVIVAL

We have been doing a great deal of preaching in this book regarding the need of taking care of patients' psychological as well as physical needs. We are aware that in order for physicians to follow through on these practices, their own psychological needs must be met. Since we try hard to be consistent, we suggest that there are rules that the physician can apply to assure personal psychological well-being. These rules were developed out of our teaching experience with residents. This is the dozen found to be most helpful in practice.

Rule 1: Do Not Take Responsibility for Things You Cannot Control

The implication of this rule is that if we did not have control of the circumstances that helped to create a situation, we cannot take responsibility for the effect that situation has on others. The practical application of this rule is that when a person complains about a situation over which *we* have no control and that we did not create, we are able to empathize with their frustration, pain, or other discomfort without becoming *defensive*. We can sympathize with patients about the inflexibility of rules made by hosptials, HMOs, or the government without feeling as though we have to do anything about it. It is a situation over which we have no control. We are not responsible for creating the patient's disease. We may or may not be able to treat it effectively.

The corollary of Rule 1 is that we must take responsibility for what we can control—our own behavior. It is a given that in order to control our behavior, we must first be aware of it and also recognize our limits.

Rule 2: Take Care of Yourself or You Can't Take Care of Anyone Else.

It is really important that physicians become aware of their own limits and tolerance for certain situations. When we find that we are going on *tilt* it is imperative that we take time out. Physicians need to learn stress management techniques, build a support group, set realistic expectations for themselves, and set limits on the demands of others (gently, of course). Becoming overstressed impairs functioning. Once functioning is impaired, the outcome becomes questionable. This leads to Rule 3.

Rule 3: Trouble Is Easier to Prevent Than to Fix

This concept needs little elaboration. Often a minute or two spent in explaining something or considering the consequences of a potential action can avoid extensive problems. Exploring potential outcomes and worst case scenarios before the fact can ultimately save time and aggravation. Doing nothing is often better than doing something, especially when all the data is not in. Applying tincture of time when hasty action might precipitate an unstoppable process is an important option to consider.

Rule 4: When You Get Upset, Tune into What Is Going on with You and Go through the Three-Step Process

1. What am I feeling?
2. What do I want?
3. What can I do about it?

This effective strategy for getting in touch with and managing feelings and behavior was presented in Chapter 7. It is an important skill for the physician to apply personally. Whenever there is a sense of starting to approach *tilt*—feeling a strong sense of being internally pressured and clearly out of sorts—we recommend tuning in and labeling the experienced feeling. Is it anger, frustration, impatience, sadness, fatigue, or what? That is step 1.

Step 2 requires getting in touch with what is actually wanted: "I want the patients to stop being so demanding." "I want my receptionist to be better organized." "I want someone to take care of me, for a change." "I want someone to acknowledge that I am trying to do a good job."

Step 3 requires figuring out what one can personally do to accomplish what is desired. If we are more sympathetic to the patients, they may actually become less demanding. The receptionist may need some support if this is an unusual style for her, or she may need to be given clear instructions, and if that is not sufficient, she may need to be replaced. As far as getting someone to take care of us is concerned, we may have to learn to ask for what we want and then to learn to accept it. Sometimes, there is nothing that we can do to get what we want. We can't get it to stop raining on our parade. We can't change the past or how someone else is feeling or reacting. That brings us to Rule 5.

Rule 5: If the Answer to Step 3, Rule 4 Is "Nothing," Apply Rule 1

Rule 1, of course, states that we should not take responsibility for things we cannot control. In this case, since there is nothing we can do to get what we want, we need to accept that. We do not beat ourselves for not being able to affect something over which we have no power. Then, recycling Rule 4 usually will result in feeling sad or wishing that it was a more perfect world. Since there is nothing that we can do to affect that, the result is usually a feeling of acceptance, smug satisfaction at being so wise, and an appreciation of ourselves and our ability to sort out feelings. Our experience has been that when we go through this process, there is generally a strong sense of taking control. By definition, this results in a sense of competence that is mutually exclusive to feeling overwhelmed. We are fixed! We feel better. It works for us as it does for patients.

Rule 6: Ask for Support When You Need It—Give People Permission to Feel What They Feel

This simple strategy affirms the importance of accepting ourselves and others where we are. We all need support sometimes, and the need does not imply weakness. Giving people permission to feel what they feel costs nothing. It implies a recognition of the fact that if they could feel differently they would.

Rule 7: In a Bad Situation You Have Four Options

1. Leave It.
2. Change it.
3. Accept it.
4. Reframe it.

This strategy was discussed at length in Chapter 8. We cannot underscore too strongly the freeing effect of learning to reframe situations. If there is nothing that we can do to change an uncomfortable circumstance, we can learn to give ourselves points for flowing with it, not upsetting ourselves, using the time to think about options for next time, or any other constructive attitude or behavior. We can turn this situation into a successful learning experience. In any case, a way to program "small wins" needs to be found. The small win may simply be, not complaining—it is futile, and would only make others uncomfortable. Finding a constructive way to look at the circumstances so that it results in a positive personal outcome, is the essense of reframing.

Rule 8: If You Never Make Mistakes, You're Not Learning Anything

Self-beating for honest, unintentional mistakes is not constructive.

Mistakes resulting from ignorance or fatigue can be reframed, once you recognize that they need to be prevented. See Rule 3.

Rule 9: When a Situation Turns out Badly, Look at Where the Choice Points Were, Then Decide What You Would Do Differently Next Time

This rule needs little explanation. Again, the aim is to get something constructive from something that cannot be changed. If there is nothing that you would change, given a chance to replay the situation, it is important to acknowledge that there is no blame, since circumstances obviously did not work out as would generally be expected. However, it is usually a good idea to reexamine any expectations as to their innate reasonableness.

Rule 10: At Any Given Time You Can Only Make Decisions Based on the Information You Have

This again was discussed in Chapter 7. The value of postponing decisions when possible, applying tincture of time, and talking things through with supportive others must be acknowledged.

Rule 11: Life Is Not Fair—or a Contest

Life really is not fair. Once we accept this fact, it gets easier. We don't even have to feel guilty about the things that we have and that people who are less fortunate do not have.

Life is also not a contest. Many people live as though it is. It helps to realize that the important things—love, healing, reaching one's potential—are on a different dimension from a zero-sum game. The more we allow ourselves and others to experience them, the more there is for all. People who feel secure have no need to put others down.

Rule 12: You Have to Start Where the Patient Is at

At any given time, a person can only be where he or she is. If they could be any different, they would be—and so would you.

SUMMARY

In taking care of hateful patients, awareness that these patients are attempting to solve problems the best way they can is helpful. Setting limits regarding time spent and number of problems discussed and reframing the situation as a learning opportunity helps the physician cope.

Hypochondriacal patients are helped by regular appointments and exploring the context of their lives along with their symptomatology. Their suffering is acknowledged and they are allowed to retain one or two symptoms. Chronic complainers are recognized as needing their disease but encouraged to make small changes that help them feel more in control of their lives.

To treat substance abusers successfully, strict limits must be set. Depressed patients must be given permission to be depressed, while being encouraged to make small changes in the circumstances of their lives. Grieving patients must be encouraged to examine the significant aspects of their terminated relationships and actively mourn their loss. They need to be encouraged to feel their pain, rather than try to shut it off.

Serious consideration of suicide generally corresponds with feelings of poor self-esteem, lack of social support, and lack of hope. The physician counters these by a show of concern and a commitment to help. A contract is made and patients' promise to call or come in at a specific time is elicited. Clear documentation and backup are required.

In dealing with family members, power struggles must be avoided and verbal aikido is used to defuse opposition. Guilt is relieved whenever possible. When having to confront patients or families, physicians are warned to expect counterattacks, retreats, or diversions.

Training the office staff in supportive psychological strategies is effective, as is adopting enlightened expectations for oneself. Rules for physician survival based on our philosophy are presented.

REFERENCES

1. *The Holy Bible*, Luke 4: 23.
2. Groves, J. E. Taking care of the hateful patient. *New England Journal of Medicine*, 1978, *298*, 883–887.
3. Adler, G. The physician and the hypochondriacal patient. *New England Journal of Medicine*, 1981, *304*, 1384–1396.

4. Barsky, A. J. and Klerman, G. L. Overview: Hypochondriasis, bodily complaints, and somatic styles. *American Journal of Psychiatry*, 1983, *140*, 273-283.

5. Watzlawick, P. *The Language of Change: Elements of Therapeutic Communication*. New York: Basic Books, 1978, p. 73.

6. Rittelmeyer, L. F., Jr. Coping with the chronic complainer. *American Family Physician*, 1985, *31*, 211-215.

7. Lipkin, M. Functional or organic? A pointless question. *Annals of Internal Medicine*, 1969, *71*, 1013-1017.

8. Pierloot, R. A. The treatment of psychosomatic disorders by the general practitioner. *International Journal of Psychiatry in Medicine*. 1977-8, *8*, 43-51.

9. Cavenar, J. O., Jr., Nash, J. L., and Maltbie, A. A. Anniversary reactions presenting as physical complaints. *Journal of Clinical Psychiatry*, 1978, *39*, 369-374.

10. Barsky, A. J. III. Patients who amplify bodily sensations. *Annals of Internal Medicine*, 1979, *91*, 63-70.

11. Lennard-Jones, J. E. Functional gastrointestinal disorders. *New England Journal of Medicine*, 1983, *308*, 431-435.

12. Monson, R. A. and Smith, G. R. Somatization disorder in primary care. *New England Journal of Medicine*, 1983, *308*, 1464-1465.

13. Smith, C. W. The irritable bowel syndrome. *The Female Patient*, 1985, *10*, 81-90.

14. Lesser, I. M. Alexithymia. *New England Journal of Medicine*, 1985, *312*, 690-692.

15. Alexander, F. Fundamental concepts of psychosomatic research: Psychogenesis, conversion, specificity. *Psychosomatic Medicine*, 1943, *5*, 205-210.

16. Fenichel, O. *The Psychoanalytic Theory of Neurosis*. New York: Norton, 1945.

17. Robertson, N. C. Variations in referral pattern to the psychiatric services by general practitioners. *Psychological Medicine*, 1979, *9*, 355-364.

18. Hull, J. The use of psychiatric referrals by non-psychiatric physicians. *Medical Care*, 1979, *17*, 718-726.

19. Brickman, P., Rabinowitz, V. C., Karusa, J., Jr. et. al. Models of helping and coping. *American Psychologist*, 1982, *37*, 368-384.

20. Klein, D. C. and Seligman, E. P. Reversal of performance deficits and perceptual deficits in learned helplessness and depression. *Journal of Abnormal Psychology*, 1976, *85*, 11-26.

21. Bornstein, P. E. and Clayton, P. J. The anniversary reaction. *Diseases of the Nervous System*, 1972, (July), *33*, 470-472.

22. Doherty, W. J. and Baird, M. A. *Family Therapy and Family Medicine*. New York: Guilford Press, 1983.

23. Palmer, J. D. Workshop on improving conflict skills. Unpublished paper, 1977.

Anticipated Outcomes

10

In promoting the art of incorporating psychotherapeutic techniques into the practice of primary care medicine, we expect that there will be outcomes that enhance the experience of the physician, the patient, the patient's family, the profession, and even society as a whole. In this chapter, we would like to discuss some of these grandiose notions.

PHYSICIAN FACTORS

Eric Erikson[1] has pointed out that each individual's social identity depends on three complementary factors: first; the personal coherence of the individual and (his or her) role integration with his group; second, the guiding images and ideologies of the time; and third, his or her personal life history and the history of the moment. For the primary care physician practicing at this particular historical moment, the choice is clear. Either one must accept the new paradigm and find ways to integrate new techniques and new insights in order to achieve both personal satisfaction and constructive patient outcomes, or one may continue to try to function according to the old medical model and experience large measures of frustration when outcomes are less than optimal, both personally and for the patient.

Professional Identity Issues

When we look at the personal coherence of the physician and the role integration with the group, it would seem clear that by applying the principles outlined in this book, the physician would be able to process and meaningfully integrate the variety of experiences that contributed to his or her professional growth and development. It will be possible to sort out the core values and important truths that originally led to choosing medicine as a career. It is important to understand how the process of medical education, undergraduate and residency training, and the pressures inherent in starting a practice may have gotten the physician off the track of providing meaningful, personal care for individual patients and enjoying a satisfying professional life. We would challenge the practitioner to examine some of the underlying assumptions of the old medical model, discarding elements that are no longer useful and recommitting to practicing with an awareness of the potential positive power inherent in the role of physician. We would propose that, by reframing, the current upheaval in the medical care delivery system can be seen as an opportunity rather than an inconvenience.

Responding to a Changed Paradigm

Buckminster Fuller's work has cast out all doubt that we can any longer say, "It is fortunate that the Good Lord created the universe exactly divided into the traditional academic disciplines."[2] Just as biochemistry has bridged the gap between biology and chemistry, biophysics has bridged the gap between biology and physics and has much to teach us about immunology. The power of imagery to affect bodily processes is demonstrated daily through biofeedback. We know that how we think determines how we feel about what is happening and that positive thoughts apparently contribute to positive outcome. We know that how we think determines how we feel and that feeling powerful or helpless affects our immune response. The most dangerous state for our body as well as for our mind exists when we feel overwhelmed.

All of this can be seen as putting a traditionally trained physician into a situation of great stress. Many of the absolutes that have formed the core of understanding are changing or have changed drastically. Dealing with changed circumstances precipitates stress. And how do people respond when under great stress? Under extreme circumstances:

1. They intensify their usual psychological and social devices that they have previously used to cope.
2. When these devices fail, they experience anger that must be repressed or else the sources of existing support could be expected to dry up more.

3. They turn on themselves, internalizing their aggressive impulses and perhaps develop feelings of guilt.
4. They no longer feel able to cope—they feel helpless and develop symptoms. The prescription at this point is to provide support, which gratifies some of the dependency needs without undermining self-respect.

We are trying to provide support. Our cookbook approach is designed to facilitate the application of some very effective techniques that will ultimately lead to optimum utilization of time, increased satisfaction, increased income, and personal growth for the physician.

Applying the Model

The questions we would pose are an application of our method. How do you feel about what is going on in the medical care delivery system today? Or, how do you feel about how you are practicing medicine today? What do you want? In other words, how do you want to practice? What can you do about it?

We would recommend that the physician be very clear about the answers to these questions. If what is wanted is that things go back to the way they were, unfortunately there is nothing that can be done about that. The road goes on. If what is desired concerns keeping up and being productive and successful, we would propose that there are many strategies in this book that will contribute to that end. By putting into practice what we have outlined, the physician will approach these goals.

Achieving Professional Success

As physicians develop a reputation for treating the whole person and providing preventive service, including anticipatory guidance, their practice will inevitably grow. With the anticipated physician glut,[3] those physicians who provide full services will be sought out by knowledgeable patients. By developing a practice based on continuity of care, with regular planned visits, and providing anticipatory guidance to an optimally sized patient population, the predictable patient flow will provide a comfortable income level for a reasonable time commitment. By monitoring stressful events in patients' lives, problems may be caught earlier and at less complicated stages.

Also, as more and more medical care is provided on a prepaid basis, there will be a financial incentive for keeping people well by preventing and limiting serious illness. However, the most important payoff for the physician may ultimately be the satisfaction of participating meaningfully and contributing to the quality of patients' lives.

Attaining Personal Growth

The final payoff for physicians adopting our techniques of psychotherapy will be their own personal growth. By applying the principles outlined in this book to their own life situation, physicians will feel empowered. It will become somewhat easier to juggle professional commitments, family obligations, and personal needs. Physicians will develop their own sense of coherence and incorporate a rational, flexible, and farsighted coping style.[4] The matrix of personal identity that must be developed includes identification of feelings about career, relationships with both patients and colleagues, personal relationships, financial and security issues, relationships to the wider community, and ultimately the meaning of life.[5] Becoming aware of the feelings related to these issues, acknowledging wants, and deciding what strategies are available for satisfying them will lead to positive personal growth. As human beings, we may be organisms affected by demands from the environment, but we are also agents, subjects who act with intentionality.

Moving Toward Self-Actualization

As needs for physical survival, security, acceptance, and achievement get met, physicians will invariably approach that part of Maslow's hierarchy of needs identified as self-actualization.[6] It will be remembered that Maslow proposed that once the basic needs are satisfied, individuals reach for higher gratifications. Self-actualized people make full use of their talents, capabilities, and potentialities. They develop to the full stature of which they are capable.

To approach self-actualization, individuals must have learned to gratify basic emotional needs for safety, belongingness, love, respect, and self-respect—and cognitively met needs for knowledge and understanding. They also need to have worked out their philosophical, religious, or axiological bearings.

Becoming self-actualized results in a more efficient perception of reality and more comfortable relations with it. Self-actualized people do not need to cling to the familiar. They are relatively comfortable with the vague and indefinite, and the quest for truth assumes priority over the need for safety. There is an acceptance of self, others, and nature. This is to be highly recommended, since it makes for serenity. Self-actualized people develop an increased ability to be spontaneous and a code of ethics that is autonomous. Self-actualized people, like good physicians, are problem centered rather than ego centered. They exhibit a certain quality of objective detachment and have a need for privacy. They rely on their own interpretation of situations. In other words, they have an internal locus of control.

Other desirable qualities that Maslow cites as characteristic of achieving self-actualization include a continued freshness of appreciation of the richness of experience, profound interpersonal relationships, development of a democratic character structure, a sense that means *are* ends, creativeness, and an unhostile sense of humor.

People are not born self-actualized. It is a state that develops through a process fostered by the type of techniques we are advocating in this book. By teaching these techniques to their patients, physicians will inevitably be positively affected.

PATIENT FACTORS

Having discussed from a broad viewpoint the potential benefits likely to accrue to the physician who incorporates psychotherapeutic techniques into the usual patient visit, let us now look at the effect on the patient.

Not Cure in the Traditional Sense

When dealing with patients' problems as outlined in this book, we do not suggest that the physician is curing in the traditional sense. It may well be that there is no such thing as a specific disease in the traditional sense or a specific cure. The particular interaction with the physician that we are proposing will help to enhance the patient's sense of well-being and support the patient's own healing powers. The patient's immune system should return to effectiveness, that is, be less compromised.[7] When the patient feels empowered, he or she will behave in ways that will result in more productive interactions with other people.

We are not claiming that we have solutions to chronic problems that have eluded other well-meaning health professionals. We only have an approach designed to improve things. For the final case example to be presented in this book, let us look at the case of Emily M., the type of patient who is characterized by a really thick chart.

> Emily M. is a 43-year-old black female with limited education who came into the office two years ago complaining of chest pain. She brought prescriptions for 13 different medications prescribed by half a dozen different doctors. She had been hospitalized numerous times for extensive workups of multiple aches and pains for which she had gone to the emergency room and been admitted. Cardiologists, pulmonologists, gastroenterologists, orthopedists, otolaryngologists, and gynecologists had each run their battery of tests from CT scans and sigmoidoscopy to coronary catherization, without elucidating the origin of her symptoms. Each added another drug to her regimen and referred her to the next specialist, until she had seen them all. Having run out of subspecialists she came to the family practice center.
>
> History revealed that the onset of her various acute pains would correspond with arguments with her abusive, alcoholic, and unemployed (disabled) husband. Overall, she presented with the affect and vegetative signs of depression. Dr. S's clinical impression was that Emily was suffering primarily from depressive and somatization disorders. He weaned her off all her medications except sublingual nitroglycerine, taught her relaxation techniques, and started her on imipramine.
>
> Emily was seen regularly, once a week for several months, during which time emphasis was shifted away from her physical pains, while her shattered living situation and social problems were explored. A social worker and a women's self-help group were involved in her case. Emily was given strict instructions to call the center when she experienced acute pain rather than going to the emergency room. During her office visits, Dr. S. attended to her physical complaints without lingering on them and then spent most of the fifteen minute session listening to the precipitating factors and new stresses in her life. He offered support and sought to focus Emily on those things that she could do to improve matters. Intervals between visits were gradually increased until they were every four weeks. At this time, she showed up in the emergency room complaining of chest pain! No acute problem was found.
>
> Visits were then scheduled at intervals ranging from every two to four weeks and she improved slowly but steadily. In contrast to

the multiple admissions in each of the previous five years, Emily has remained out of the hospital for the past two years, except for one hospitalization for hypotonic bowel with partial obstruction at the time of her sister's death. She continues to be seen at regular intervals, and although her living situation is no better, she is functioning at a somewhat higher level than before.

In every case, our goals involve helping patients to achieve whatever potential is reasonable for them, at *this time*. For Emily to stay out of the hospital for two years is an enormous accomplishment. Although functioning less than optimally by society's standards, her current level of adaptation is nonetheless remarkable.

Realizing One's Own Potential

Rather than engaging patients in a relationship that fosters dependency, we encourage them to realize their own potential. We focus on their strengths and make them aware that they are at all times exercising choices. We point out that there are always options. We encourage them to make the best possible choice at any given time. The implication is that the physician and the patient are on the same side—the patient's. It is through the partnership with the physician that patients achieve the confidence to act positively in their own interest.

Enhancing Health

It is generally accepted today that the patient's health is largely determined by what the patient does, that is, the type of life style that the patient adopts rather than what happens during a visit to a physician's office. We do not intend to quarrel about this, but instead we want to encourage the use of strategies and techniques that will enhance the physician's ability to affect the patient's behavior or choice of life style in a positive way. When a physician provides the type of care that we are advocating, patients' satisfaction and compliance with physician's instructions will be greatly enhanced.[8]

When a patient is somatizing and the physician inquires about what is going on in the patient's life, some skeptics may still contend that an uninitiated patient may object to this change of focus.

Patient: "You mean it's all in my mind?"

Physician: "No, not at all. Your body is telling you that you are under stress and really hurting."

We want patients to start listening to their bodies, to monitor themselves and become aware of the precursors to *tilt* and to ease the pressure on themselves without having to become sick.

In actuality, many patients are requesting that physicians get involved in the emotional and social aspects of their health and disease processes.[9] When patients are able to accept and utilize the support provided by the physician, we can expect positive health consequences. Their sense of well-being will be enhanced. We can also expect increased resistence to stresses of all kinds. They may be less susceptible to infections of various sorts, less accident prone, and handle life's stresses in more constructive ways. They will solve problems more productively. They will become aware of the impact of their own reactions on others and on the things that happen to them. This type of constructive adaptation can be expected to lead to better physical and mental health.

The secondary prevention implicit in our model of practice is even more directly measurable. Since illness itself generally upsets the balance of psychosocial well-being for patients and their families, the prevention of complications from the illness for patient and family is clear. People are encouraged to engage their most constructive coping mechanisms, feel supported, and get their needs met on an ongoing basis rather than having care givers only responding to a series of catastrophes. The type of trust built by being cared for and cared about will enhance patients' sense of basic trust in the world (the sense of coherence), which should result in improved health consequences.[2]

Improving Relationships

When patients apply the types of personal strategies that we have outlined, their relationships within their families, work settings, and the community in general can be expected to improve. As we encourage people to feel less helpless, they will resist being exploited and also have less of a need to exploit others. Communication patterns should become more open and direct and problems handled in more productive ways. Much of this may sound utopian, but we have shown the powerful effect of small wins and the importance of supporting people so that they can function in their healthy, rather than their neurotic, mode. People who are acting from their healthy map of the world have positive expectations about their relationships with others, which then become self-fulfilling prophecies.

EFFECTS ON THE FAMILY

It is obvious from the above that improved patient functioning must improve the situation of other family members. We are aware of complicated family dynamics, old conflicts, and competing and seemingly mutually exclusive opinions, agendas, and desires. Although family interventions are beyond the scope of this book, since the patient is a member of a system—*and every part of a system is connected to and reciprocally affects every other part of the system*—as we encourage the patient to change certain behaviors, there will be corresponding effects on other family members. Ultimately, this can have a positive effect on everyone.

Additional Consequences of Improved Patient Functioning

By encouraging patients to communicate more clearly and directly, they and the other members of their family will have less need to manipulate each other by becoming sick or engaging in various destructive behaviors. As patients apply the practical child management techniques that we have advocated, it can be expected that their children will grow up with a relatively well-formed sense of security, feeling both competent and lovable.

Here again we have engaged a benevolent circle, the essence of primary prevention. People who have an enhanced sense of health and well-being can be expected to treat other people with consideration and respect. They will engage their healthy map of the world and the other people in it.

IMPLICATIONS FOR THE PROFESSION

It is no secret that there is a growing public dissatisfaction with the medical profession. Hardly a day goes by without a reference in the lay press to either the method of health care delivery or the cost of medical care. Public dissatisfaction with the medical profession is not a new phenomenon. In fact, it was one of the major reasons for the establishment of the American Medical Association in the first place.[10] Over time, there has been some ebb and flow in the level of satisfaction. In the middle of this century, with all the advances being made by modern medicine, there was something akin to a flood tide resulting in a national romance with the medical profession.[11] This contention was supported by the popularity of many of the medical television programs and motion pictures of that era. Didn't everyone want Dr. Marcus Welby to be their own personal physician, with Ben Casey as his consultant? It's a shame, but the love affair has ended.

Currently there seems to be more ebb than flow in the tide of satisfaction with the medical profession. We believe, as does Engel,[12] that much of this problem can be traced to the method of educating medical practitioners. As we stressed in Chapter 1, the dualism that separates mind from body and the reductionistic approach to medical problem solving effectively isolate the disease from the patient and the patient from the physician, when in reality they are inexorably linked.

By adopting our approach to the patient, the physician demonstrates the ability to integrate the psyche and the soma in a way that will convince the patient that, in fact, this physician is indeed interested in more than just biological processes; this physician is interested in the patient as a person. There is no question that the physician must be eminently skilled in dealing with traditional medical problems, but to deal with only the organic is to deal incompletely with the patient. We feel equally strongly that by employing the techniques presented in this book, the physician will be able to respond to all the needs that are traditionally brought by a patient to a physician. This will improve the physician's effectiveness and image. Among other benefits, this will place the physician in a much better position in our increasingly litigious society. Patients do not sue physicians with whom they have a relationship of mutual trust, respect, and caring. Norman Cousins suggests that doctors who spend more time with their patients may have to spend less money on malpractice protection.[13] Although we agree, we are more concerned about the quality of the time spent with the patient than the quantity.

SOCIETAL IMPLICATIONS

As stated in *Healthy People: The Surgeon General's Report on Health*

Promotion and Disease Prevention,[14] prevention is an idea whose time has come. It is imperative that we focus on prevention for a number of good reasons—prevention saves lives, improves the quality of life, and is economical in the long run.

Promoting Health

In the sections on healthy children, adolescents, and young adults, the focus of the *Surgeon General's Report* is on the home environment and the quality of interactions with parents that foster and promote emotional, mental, and physical health.[15] The *Report* points out that physical and mental health are linked and enhanced through maintenance of strong family ties and social support. We are suggesting that the physician can play an important role in facilitating these important factors.

Of course, not everyone can be healthy. Disease and disability will inevitably be experienced by all people. However, predispositions based on hereditary or socioeconomic factors are mediated by individual experience to include the environmental and behavioral factors capable of provoking ill health with or without previous predisposition. Emotional stress is one of the factors cited in the report as being related to serious illnesses such as heart disease and cancer.

Focusing on Mental Health

The President's Commission on Mental Health reported that in 1975 fully 3 percent of the U.S. population (almost seven million people) sought treatment from specialists in mental health. It was also noted that a large proportion of patients who were treated by nonpsychiatrists had some emotional or psychiatric problems. This report indicated that at any given time 25 percent of the population is estimated to be "suffering from mild to moderate depression, anxiety, or other emotional disorder."[16] Anything that can be done to minimize this distress must be promoted.

Focusing on the Elderly

In discussing elderly patients, the *Surgeon General's Report* emphasized not only the contribution of social and psychological factors, such as abrupt and unwanted changes faced by the elderly and their relation to physical health, but cited depression as a significant and potentially devastating problem in the elderly.[17] The primary care physician who incorporates psychotherapy into everyday medical practice is in a unique position to make a meaningful impact here. The aging of our population provides a strong mandate to get involved with the whole patient and help promote small wins.

Controling Stress

Stress control is listed as one of the major goals of health promotion.[18] This includes both reducing levels of stress and the consequences resulting from experiencing high levels of stress. Two strategies must be employed, one to reduce actual stress and one to modify reactions and enhance coping skills. Responsibility for implementing these strategies is in the hands of the health care professional who first sees the people at risk. The importance of starting with a clear understanding of the type of events that are most difficult for the individual to handle is cited.

PUTTING HEALTH PROMOTION AND DISEASE PREVENTION INTO PRACTICE

It can be seen from the above that there is a clear mandate for the primary care physician, as part of health maintenance functions, to screen for stress-related problems and help patients manage their reactions to the events in their lives in the most constructive way possible. We have tried to outline how this can be done. At the minimum, each patient can be BATHEd and given permission to feel whatever feelings are being experienced. Limited information about how people react to stress can be imparted and specific suggestions given for managing stress effectively. Anticipatory guidance can be given to minimize stress inherent in adjusting to expected transitions. Physicians can learn to ask questions that focus patients on their own strengths. The appendix has a brief list of very effective questions and excellent responses with which to start to accomplish these goals.

SUMMING UP

A final word. Can psychotherapy, as we have proposed it be practiced, really work? It always has. It used to be called moral treatment.

Moral treatment was practiced in the United States during the nineteenth century, before Sigmund Freud, Jung, Adler, Wilhelm Wundt, Pavlov, Skinner, Dollard, Miller, Bateson, Perls, Bandura, Beck, or Ellis. Long before any of us were thought of, moral treatment aimed to prevent, treat, and correct various causes of mental disorders. Therapy consisted of creating a milieu in which the emphasis was on building up the self-esteem and self-control of the patient through the judicious use of "rewards and punishments in the context of a strong emotional relationship with a doctor."[19]

We think it's a great idea for the twentieth and twenty-first centuries, expecially when we can incorporate the contributions of those other giants and stand on their shoulders so that we can see further and more clearly. Certainly, it will enhance the health of the patient and the health, happiness, and image of the practicing primary care physician.

REFERENCES

1. Erikson, E. *Life History and the Historical Moment*. New York: Norton, 1975.
2. Fuller, R. B. *Synergistics*. New York: Macmillan, 1975.
3. U. S. Dept. of Health and Human Services. *Summary Report of the Graduate Medical Educational National Advisory Committee*. Washington, D. C.: U. S. Government Printing Office, 1980.
4. Antonovsky, A. *Health, Stress, and Coping*. San Francisco: Jossey-Bass, 1979.
5. Schmiedeck, R. A. The sense of identity and the role of continuity and confluence. *Psychiatry*, 1979, *43*, 157–164.
6. Maslow, A. H. Self-actualizing people: A study of psychological health. *Personality*, 1950, Symposium 1, 11–34.
7. Ader, R., ed. *Psychoneuroimmunology*. New York: Academic Press, 1981.
8. Ley, P. Satisfaction, compliance and communication. *British Journal of Clinical Psychology*, 1982, *21*, 241–254.
9. Fiore, N. Fighting cancer—one patient's perspective. *New England Journal of Medicine*, 1979, *300*, 284–289.
10. Starr, P. *The Social Transformation of American Medicine*. New York: Basic Books, 1984, p. 424.
11. Lieberman, J. A. III, Family medicine and the aging patient: Clinical and educational issues. *New Jersey Family Physician*, 1984, 8, 28–33.
12. Engel, G. L. The clinical application of the biopsychosocial model. *The American Journal of Psychiatry*, 1980, *137*, 535–544.

13. Cousins, N. *The Healing Heart.* New York: Norton, 1983, p. 162.

14. *Healthy People: The Surgeon General's Report on Health Promotion and Disease Prevention,* DHEW (PHS) Publ. No. 79-55071. U. S. Dept of HEW, Public Health Service, 1979.

15. Ibid, p. 42.

16. Ibid, p. 68.

17. Ibid, p. 77.

18. Ibid, pp. 135-138.

19. Freedman, A. M., Kaplan, H. I., and Sadock, B. J. *Modern Synopsis of Comprehensive Textbook of Psychiatry II,* 2nd ed. Baltimore: Williams & Wilkins, 1976, p. 22.

Appendix

A DOZEN GOOD QUESTIONS AND THREE GOOD ANSWERS FOR ALL SEASONS

Questions that have therapeutic value:

1. How do you feel about that?
2. What troubles you the most?
3. How are you handling that?
4. What are you feeling right now?
5. What do you want?
6. What can *you* do about that?
7. What are your options?
8. What's the best thing that can happen?
9. What's the worst thing that can happen?
10. What's in it for you?
11. What does it mean to you?
12. What, specifically, do you want from me?

Responses that have therapeutic value:

1. That must be very difficult for you.
2. I can understand that you would feel that way.*
3. Under the circumstances, I'm sure that you (he, she, they) did the best you (he, she, they) could.

---

*Not to be confused with "I understand how you feel," or, "I know how you feel," which are *not* recommended, since they may lead to arguments. No one can really know how another person is feeling.

Index

acceptance: achieving feeling of, 169–170; physician's effect on patient, 142–143
accidents, correlation with anniversaries, 117
acting out, 26
acute illness, as acute stress, 29
adaptation: poor, relation to poor health, 25; successful, 25; theories, 24–29
advice, 143–147
affective response, encouraging, 117–118
aikido, verbal, 161, 172
Alcoholics Anonymous, 73, 98
Alexander, Franz, 156
alternate interpretations of situations, exploring, 140–142
altruism, 26
Angyal, Andras, 27
anniversary, significance of, 117
anniversary reactions, 160
anticipation, 26
Antonovsky, Aaron, 23
anxiety, related to physical complaint, 21
anxiety models, 63–65
approach-approach, precipitation of anxiety, 63, 77
approach-avoidance, precipitation of anxiety, 63, 77
Argyris, Chris, 28
arousal, levels of, 28
assertiveness training, 63, 145
attention, healing in, 49
attitudes, mechanisms of changing, 43–44
authority: ambivalence toward, 45; response, 93
autonomy, drive for, 27

avoidance-avoidance, precipitation of anxiety, 63, 77

balance of power, shifting, 123
Balint, Michael, 89
BATHE, 102–104, 113, 120, 126, 130, 154, 185
behavior: ABCs, 65; approval or acceptance of, 22; distinguishing from thoughts and feelings, 146; extinguishing, 65; strategies to promote new, 94
behavioral options, examining, 140
behavioral repertoire, 91
behavior therapy, 62–63
benevolent circle, engagement, 182
benzodiazepines, 38
bereavement, mortality risk, 11
biofeedback, 63, 175
biomedical model, paradigm, 14
biomedical model of illness, 7
biopsychosocial model, 17
blame, 71
breast cancer, prognosis, 11
Brickman, Philip, 71
brief sessions, effects, 96–97

Caplan, Gerald, 31, 104, 111
cardiovascular disease, links with behavioral factors, 12
care, taking of oneself, 145–146
caring: gift, 86–87; nonpossessive, 77
caring attitude, communicating, 48–50
Castelnuovo-Tedesco, P., 90
change, decision, 59
changing situation, 141, 150
children, behavioral management, 144–145
choosing, not to choose, 121, 122–123

chronic conditions, stress as exacerbation, 116
client-centered therapy, 62, 119
coercive power, 44
cognitive interventions, 157
cognitive services, compensation, 6
coherence, health promoting, 132
commitment, physician, 92
community practitioners, referral, 98
compensatory model, 72-73, 77; chronic problems, 106-107, 113; fostering of self-esteem, 108
complainers, chronic, 155-158
compliance: relation to identification, 45; role of coercive power in 44
conflict, family members, 163
conflict resolution, strategies for, 92
confrontation, 163-165
connectedness, restoration of sense of, 57
consequences, looking at, 121-122
conservation of funds for care, 7
contact, early phase, 96
continuity, physician-patient relationship, 40-41, 99
contract for caring and concern, 60
control, 71; loss of, 24
corrective experiences, 60-61
counseling, 132
Cousins, Norman, 12, 15, 38, 183
crisis, definition, 31; resolution, 32
crisis intervention, goals, 32
crisis intervention model, 31-33
crisis theory, 111
cure traditional, 178

data gathering, 48
decision making, clinical, 8
decompensating, 26
defense mechanisms, 26
defusing defensiveness, 162
deleting, 68
delusional projection, 26
dependency needs, medical model in satisfying, 108
dependent clingers, 152
dependent mode, 30
depressed patient, 158-159, 172
depression, permission, 159
desensitization, 63
diagnosis, psychiatry, 80
diary keeping, 97
disease, illness without, 14
disenchantment, public with medical profession, 13
distorting sensory data, 68
doctor-patient relationship, identification of problem, 5

Eagleton case, 81
economic considerations, 6-7
8-week limit, uneffectiveness, 38
elderly patients, 184-185
Ellis, Albert, 66
emotional disorder, prevalence, 184
emotional illness, physician role in, 84
emotional problems, scheduling patients, 118
emotional response, unexpected, 104
empathetic statement, 134
empathy: accurate, 77; giving, 92-93; with patient's experience, family knowledge role, 85
employment application, mental, emotional disorder query, 81
Engel, George, 8, 15, 16, 17
enlightened model, 73, 77
entitled demanders, 153
environment: adaptation to, 88; external and internal, 30
Erikson, Eric, 174
expectations of behavior, patient vs. physician, 22

experimental psychology, research from, 27–28
expert power, 45–46
explanations, 94–95
exploitation, 181
explorative therapy, 57–59
external perspective, 60
etiology and therapy, reductionistic approach, 8

family: collateral visits, 137–139, 150; effects of improved patient functioning, 182; involving patient, 91–92, 99; knowledge of, 85
family members, difficult, 161–163
family therapy, 98
feelings: distinguishing from thoughts and behavior, 146; probing for, 135–136, 150; taking responsibility for, 147
financial constraints on practice, 5
Frank, Jerome, 58, 59, 74
Fuller, Buckminster, 175

Gaylin, Willard, 86
generalization, 67
Glasser, William, 69
Grant Study of Adult Development, 25, 31
Great Society, 6
grief reactions, 114
grieving patient, 112, 159–160
growth, personal physician, 177
guidance, anticipatory, 95
guilt: compensatory model application, 74; defusing, 162–163

hateful patients, 152–153, 172
headaches, tension, 107
healing power, physician mobilization of, 15
health: enhancing, 180; maintenance of in face of stress, 23

helping and coping, models, 70–74
help-seeking behavior, trigger, 127
here and now, focus on, 89–91
historical roots, 124
holistic approach based on scientific method, 15–17
homework assignment, 97, 147–148; reporting, 134–139
homonomy, 27
humor, 26
hypertension, behavioral treatment, 12
hypochondriacal patient, 154–155, 172
hypochondriases, 26

identification with physician, 47
illness behavior stress, 28–29
immune response, 175
immune system, compromise, 24
information, internalization, 43
informational needs, cause of physician visit, 10
insight, 58
intellectualization, 26
intensive therapy, 76
interviewing skills, 52–53
irresponsibility, 69

James, William, 29

key phrases for acknowledgment of patient's response to stressful situations, 22
Kuhn, Thomas, 13, 14

language, role in therapy, 67–69
large-scale solutions, 109
learned helplessness, 30
legitimate power, 45
leverage points, minor, 109
life situation, routine inquiries, 115–117

life stress, cause for physician visit, 10
limited information, 75
listening attentively, 135
list making, 97
locus of control, 24
Lown, Bernard, 12
lymphocyte function, in spouses of breast cancer patients, 11

malpractice, 183
manipulative help-rejectors, 152
map of the world, 27
medical knowledge, half-life, 38
medical model, 73, 77, 113; acute problems, 107–108, 113; limits of traditional, 7–9, 175
medical model of disease, anomalies, 14
medical practice, goals, 176
medical profession, public dissatisfaction, 182–183
medical record, problem-oriented, 102
medical treatment, incorporating, 137
medication: discussing changes, 137; role, 106
medicine: American, changes in, 5; decline in the relevance of traditional, 13–15; new paradigm of, 16–17
mental patients, self-definition, 81, 98
Milgram, Stanley, 93
mobilization for action, biological, 19
model for understanding reaction to stress, 20–21
models of helping and coping application, 74
moral model, 72, 77
moral treatment, 186

multiple problems, 104–106
myocardial infarction, psychosocial influences on mortality, 12

Naisbitt, John, 88
negative experiences of self, 29
Nemiah, John, 87
neurosis, holistic theory, 26–27
neurotic defenses, 26
nurturance, physicians as providers, 41

office, patients and staff, 166–167
office setting, application, 33–34
office staff, training, 165–167
office visit: helping patients cope with stress related to, 21; nature of, 9–10
openness to supportive statements, 86
options: exploring, 93–94, 113; focusing on, 121–123; for handling bad situation, 141, 150; physician's assumption of existence, 143
organic disorders, cause for physician visits, 10
organizational psychology, 28
outcomes, patient factors, 178–182
overload, 96
overwhelmed feeling, 29–31

paradigm, responding to changed, 175–176
pathology, psychiatrist search for, 80
patient(s): dealing with difficult, 152–165; family, involving, 91–92; reactions of, 117–121; request for help, 81; supporting, 104
patient control through physician support, 127–129

Index

patient strength, focus, 91
payoffs, in social exchange, 42
peptic ulcers, mechanism, 12
Perls, Fritz, 22
permission, 75
personality change, physicians, 90
phone calls, fielding, 165–166
physical health, relationship to psychological health, 11–12
physician: acquisition of new skills, 5; as possessors of manifest power, 43; primary care, psychotherapeutic qualifications, 39–41; as therapist, 37
physician factors, 174–178
physician-patient relationship, 85–87
placebo effect, 15
PLISSIT, 74–76, 77, 126
positive cycle, engaging, 128
potential, realizing one's own, 180
power: attributed vs. manifest, 42–43; issue of, 41–47
power struggle, 157; adolescent, 144
prescription, as end point, 9
present, focusing patient in, 124–126, 139–142, 150
prevention, societal implications, 184
primary care, definition, 37
primary prevention, 96
primitive defenses, 26
priorities, setting, 96–97
problem(s): chronic and acute, 106–108; physician's view, 88–92
problem patients, 110
problems of living, 115
problem solving, three-step, 126–127, 130
procedural services, rewards, 6
professional identity issues, 174–175
projection, 26
psychiatric disorders, cause for physician visit, 10

psychiatric evaluation process, evaluation, 85
psychiatric labels, 98
psychiatrist: differences with primary care physician, 80; narrow focus, 88; referral, 98
psychoanalytically oriented psychotherapies, 70
psychodynamic theories, 70
psychological health, relationship to physical, 11
psychological problems, training physicians to manage, 38
psychosocial context, protocol for exploration, 50–51
psychosomatic symptoms, result of feelings, 118
psychotherapeutic contract, 110–111
psychotherapeutic intervention, 110
psychotherapeutic modalities, major contributions of, 61
psychotherapeutic techniques: in primary care, effectiveness, 37; shared elements, 59–61
psychotherapy: vs. counseling, 132; dropout rate, 81; effective elements of, 55; physician as primary source, 37
psychotic defenses, 26

rational emotive therapy, 66
reaction: legitimizing, 49; physician acceptance, 142
reaction formation, 26
reality, limited patient interpretation, 119
reality testing, 61
reality therapy, 69
records, as providers of continuity, 41
referent power, 45
referral, 97–98; preference for primary physician care, 83

reframing situation, 141, 150
regression, stress related, 26
reinforcement, variable schedules of, 65
rejection, patient interpretation of, 83–84
relationships, improving, 181
relaxation, 63
renumeration, per patient or family over time, 7
repression, 26
response pattern, breaking, 124
response set, 91
responsibility: anxiety decrease, 74; patient, 128
reward power, 44
reward system, 6
Rogers, Carl, 62, 77, 92, 118,119
run-on patient, 139–140

salutogenic model, 23
Saxe, John Godfrey, 2
scientific method vs. patient needs, 10–11
scoring system, 129, 130
secondary prevention, 96, 181
self-actualization, physician, 177–178
self-destructive deniers, 153
self-esteem, lowered level of, 22
self-exploration, patient desire to further, 82
self-help, lead of lay public in fostering, 13
self-responsibility, trend toward, 89
Selye, Hans, 19
session(s): determining number, 111–112; ending, 147
sickness triggers, 116
situation: leaving, 141, 150; physician acceptance, 142
skills, building on existing, 47–50
sleeper effect, 46
small wins, 108–110, 113, 133, 170

social isolation, cause for physician visit, 10
social power, 41–42
social support, definition, 20
societal implications, 183–185
solvability of problem, 112
somatization disorders, 156
specific suggestions, 76
staff, support of, 167
Starr, Paul, 7
starting where patient is, 135
stimuli, novel, treated as previously experienced, 28
strategy(ies): irrational beliefs, 66; physician presents to patient, 121
strength(s): focusing on, 128; patient's, 91
stress: identifying causes, 107; psychological or social, illness triggers, 116; related to office visit, 21; resistance to effects, 23; and social support, 19–21; varying adaptations to, 23–24
stress control, outcomes, 185
stress-illness relation, 19
stress management: physician, 168; techniques, 107
stressor, diagnosis by physician, 49
stress reduction techniques, 108
stress related to office visit, causes, 21–22
stress-response syndrome, 31
sublimation, 26
substance abuser, 158, 172
success, professional, 176–177
suicidal patient, 111, 160–161; support mobilization, 161
supportiveness, physician interest, 116–117
supportive therapy, 57
suppression, 26
survival, rules for physician, 167–171

symbolism, effects, 123–124, 130
symptoms: most common, 56; treatment without psychiatric labeling, 82
symptom tolerance, enhancing, 51
systems, interrelationship of, 16
Szasz, Thomas, 82

tertiary prevention, 96
therapeutic approach(es), 56, 92–93
therapeutic change, prerequisite, 92–93
therapeutic milieu, 102
therapeutic process, first positive step, 81
therapeutic relationship, 60
therapy: defining structure, 101–102; goals, 56–59; roles of patient and physicians, 81–87; small doses, 83, 98
thinking, as modifiable behavior, 63
thoughts distinguishing from feelings and behavior, 146
threshold, behavior, 28

time: allocating, 148–149; efficacy of, 112
tincture of time, 121, 122, 168, 171
transference relationship, 91
treatment, concurrent physical and psychological, 84
trust, in psychotherapeutic relationship, 39–40

ubiquity statements, 94
unexpected reactions, 120
unresolved remnant, 155

Vaillant, George, 25, 26
Valium, 106
visit(s): determining context, 50–51, 102–104; series to elicit information, 85
visualization, 63

wallowing, permitted, 125
wellness programs, 5
world view, assumptive, 55, 57

zap, response to, 164

About the Authors

Marian R. Stuart received her Ph.D. in Social/Personality Psychology from Rutgers University in 1975, having worked her way through graduate school as a clinician at the Rutgers Mental Health Center. She continued her career in community mental health, splitting her time between outpatient therapy and providing consultation and education services. In 1976 she was licensed by the State of New Jersey as a Practicing Clinical Psychologist and also received a part-time appointment in the Department of Psychiatry UMDNJ—Rutgers Medical School (presently UMDNJ—Robert Wood Johnson Medical School), teaching interviewing skills to physicians' assistants. Since joining the Department of Family Medicine in 1978 she has headed the behavioral science program, developing and teaching counseling skills especially oriented to primary care physicians. Currently a Clinical Associate Professor, Dr. Stuart's interests and publications cover a broad spectrum in medical education and behavioral science. They include faculty education, geriatrics, group dynamics, and conflict resolution. She maintains a small private practice as a clinical psychologist, but her primary commitment is to teaching the integration of mental and physical health for physicians and patients.

Joseph A. Lieberman, III received his undergraduate degree from Georgetown University and his M.D. from Jefferson Medical College of Thomas Jefferson University. His graduate training was done at Sacred Heart Hospital at Allentown, Pennsylvania, following which he spent two years as a medical officer in the United States Air Force. After completing his service obligation he practiced family medicine in Allentown for ten years and then joined the faculty of the Department of Family Medicine at the University of Medicine and Dentistry of New Jersey-Rutgers Medical School. He was named Chairman of the department in 1982 and is a full professor of family medicine. A frequent contributor to medical literature, Dr. Lieberman is also involve in numerous professional organizations. He is a Fellow of the American Academy of Family Physicians, and the Academy of Medicine of New Jersey and he is certified by the American Board of Family Practice. He is currently serving as President of the New Jersey Academy of Family Physicians.